LIVING
at the
END
of the
AGES

Apocalyptic Expectation
in the Radical Reformation

Walter Klaassen

UNIVERSITY
PRESS OF
AMERICA

Lanham • New York • London

Institute for Anabaptist and
Mennonite Studies
Conrad Grebel College
Waterloo, Ontario

Co-published by arrangement with the Institute for
Anabaptist and Mennonite Studies

Library of Congress Cataloging-in-Publication Data

Klaassen, Walter, 1926-
Living at The End of The Ages :
Apocalyptic Expectation in the Radical Reformation
/ by Walter Klaassen.
p. cm.
Includes bibliographical references and index.
1. Eschatology—History of doctrines—16th century.
2. Anabaptists.   3. Apocalyptic literature—History and criticism.
I. Title.
BT819.5.K63   1992   236' .09'031—dc20   91-38015 CIP

ISBN 0-8191-8506-X (cloth : alk. paper)
ISBN 0-8191-8507-8 (pbk. : alk. paper)

 The paper used in this publication meets the minimum requirements of
American National Standard for Information Sciences—Permanence
of Paper for Printed Library Materials, ANSI Z39.48–1984.

Dedication:

To my family
      RUTH, my wife of 40 years;
      FRANK, MICHAEL, and PHILIP, our sons;
      ELIZABETH, our daughter-in-law;
      all five of them probing, critical, and lively
      students of the *litterae humaniores*

Acknowledgements

Chapters II - VI were first given as the MENNO SIMONS LECTURES at Bethel College, North Newton, Kansas, on 30 and 31 October, and 1 November, 1988.

Chapter I was first published in *Visions and Realities* ed. H. Loewen and A. Reimer, Winnipeg: Hyperion Press, 1985, and is used by permission.

Table of contents

Foreword

Much attention has been given in recent years to apocalyptic expectation in western Europe in the late Middle Ages. Especially important is the work of Herbert Grundmann, Marjorie Reeves and Bernard McGinn. Similar attention has also focused on Puritan England in the work of Christopher Hill, Richard Bauckham, Katharine Firth, Bernard Capp and Paul Christianson.

But there has been relatively little synoptic study of apocalyptic expectation in the sixteenth century. Works on the eschatology of the Reformers have appeared, but so far there is no general study on popular apocalyptic imaginings. This work represents a beginning in filling that gap.

As will be seen, apocalyptic was a vital force in the history of Christianity from the beginning. The term as used here must be distinguished from the more inclusive term eschatology. It refers specifically to the imagining and depicting of those endtime events which were expected to take place on earth prior to the return of Christ, the Last Judgment, and the end of time.

It is difficult enough to deal with the apocalyptic schemata of one person, for instance, Joachim of Fiore. That difficulty is magnified many times when trying to describe the endtime expectation of a movement or movements as is the case with the Radical Reformation. The approach to the data and the arrangement of the final product reflects this difficulty. Instead of the chronological, I have chosen the thematic approach. Chapters II, IV, V and VI are discussions of major themes suggested by the data. I have tried to show that these themes were standard components of apocalyptic speculation from at least the 12th century onwards, and that therefore the apocalyptic of the Radical Reformation cannot be understood apart from its medieval antecedents. Chapter III brings brief biographical descriptions of four of the sixteenth century *dramatis personae*, describing the nature of their visions of the future and how they developed. It is an attempt to introduce the story of individual flesh and blood into what is a piece of intellectual history. Chapter I is a description of christian apocalyptic prior to the sixteenth century. Without it sixteenth century endtime expectation could hardly be understood.

The limitation of the subject of this book to apocalyptic means that those Radical Reformation figures who held to the quieter eschatology of waiting for Christ's return such as Andreas Carlstadt, Hans Denck, Balthasar Hubmaier, Pilgram Marpeck, Menno Simons, and Sebastian Franck, do not get much attention.   There is no attempt in this work to depict the whole of the eschatology of the Radical Reformation. The subjects of the Parousia, the Last Judgment, of death and resurrection, are therefore not specifically dealt with.

I draw the reader's attention to specialized studies by myself and other authors that have already appeared in print. The specifics will be found in the bibliography.

I wish here also to acknowledge my dependence on all who have worked at the topics discussed in this book.   In particular I express my thanks to Norman Cohn and Christopher Hill for graciously receiving me and allowing me to benefit from their understanding by answering my questions, and to Ernst Benz, now deceased.   I thank the librarians of the British Library for providing me promptly with both primary and secondary literature down to the most obscure periodical.   I am grateful to libraries in Göttingen, Utrecht, and London for providing me with photocopies of medieval and Reformation pamphlets.   For years I depended on my colleagues at Conrad Grebel College as a sounding board for ideas and hypotheses on the subjects of the book.   My gratitude to them.   In particular I am obligated to acknowledge the careful work of Mr. Sam Steiner of the Institute of Anabaptist and Mennonite Studies at Conrad Grebel College in preparing the manuscript for publication, and the Institute for undertaking to see the manuscript to publication.

Finally, my thanks to Bethel College for inviting me to deliver the major part of this book as the Menno Simons Lectures in 1988. That invitation was the necessary stimulus for getting my research of a decade into the organized form in which, essentially, it is presented here.

December, 1990.

Introduction

Human beings have always been fascinated by the realm of the fantastic. Monsters and dragons are found in the earliest human writings. No person had ever seen a dragon larger than the ten foot komodo dragon-lizard of Indonesia, but dragons that devastated countries and ate knights in armour plus their horses for lunch are the stuff of fairy tales. The mythologies of the world are filled with flying horses, sphinxes, sea monsters, great serpents, male and female demons, and composite dreadfuls of all kinds. It is therefore not at all odd that the Jewish and Christian imaginings about the time of the end of the world, the end of history, should be full of such creatures and full of gigantic events that dwarf any human experience in history. Today our imaginations are full of science fiction images of anthropoid insects and monsters and humanoid computers and space ships travelling at the speed of light. But almost always, today as then, the greatest attention is given to these creatures as expressions of evil powers determined to destroy all that is good in human life.

A very good reason for the presence of monsters and superhuman powers in the Christian imagination is that the Bible provides them for us. In the books of Daniel, Ezekiel, II Esdras, and Revelation they are part of the procession of endtime events preceding the passing away of historical time along with the old earth and the old heaven.

If Christians had studied chapters 40-55 of Isaiah or the Sermon on the Mount with the same curiosity and relentlessness they have given to the books of Daniel and Revelation, at least Christianity might have turned out differently and perhaps that part of the world most affected by Christianity also. Only too often, over the centuries, preoccupation with these books has brought out the worst in Christians. They have found in them justification for vengeance, for hating others who are identified as God's enemies, and, worst of all, taking out of God's hands the vengeance which, the Scriptures say he has reserved for himself.

The host of modern interpreters[1] of these ancient books seem not to be aware that they are but the latest in a very long series of claimants to provide us with the sure interpretation of the word of prophecy.   Never, they keep telling us have the signs of the approaching End been clearer and more obvious, never have so many of them come together, never have so many Christians been looking up for the drawing near of their salvation.   If they studied the history of the expectation of the endtimes they would learn that what they claim for our day has been claimed by equally dedicated, equally qualified, and equally inspired interpreters of prophecy in every generation of Christians since the time of Jesus.   In every generation the signs have been there, in every generation they have come together, every generation of Christians has looked up waiting for the final salvation.   Interpreters in every generation have known the meaning of the variety of beasts, monsters, angels, signs, of the seven churches, of 666.   In every generation there have been those who calculated the times and seasons, and lo and behold! they pointed unerringly to their own time!   Interpreters in every generation have confidently identified both those who were faithful and therefore could look forward to ruling with Christ, as well as the enemies of God who would be exterminated in God's terrible judgment.   And finally, in virtually every generation interpreters set to work again to recalculate and reinterpret when they were proven wrong.   And so far, after nearly 2000 years of trying, every single one of those calculations has been wrong!

But lest the impression be created that everyone who in the past was concerned with the events of the End read Daniel and the Revelation as detailed histories written in advance, it is important to mention also the many who did not take that view.   There was, in the first place, the great Augustine and his followers like the medieval bishop Otto von Freising, who interpreted these provocative books symbolically.   The sign of the End, the Antichrist, and the apostasy of Christian leaders, they said, are always with us.   We all, constantly, live in the time of the End.   Some Anabaptists too, took this view. Even the sixteenth century self-proclaimed prophecy expert, the Swabian furrier Melchior Hoffman, interpreted much of the book of Revelation symbolically and not literally.   So did the friend and critic of Anabaptism, Caspar Schwenckfeld.   But even these people used the powerful images of monsters and dragons and demigods as a way of speaking about the great, final cosmic battle between good and evil.   For all without exception believed that the end of human history was approaching and that it would come with a storm and

---

[1]For example Lindsey 1970 and 1984.

fire and destruction. Only after the storm would eternal peace and tranquility come.

The sixteenth century was, like the present, a time of feverish preoccupation with the approaching End of all things. There were only a few writers of that time for whom the issue was of no interest, the two most notable examples being the great humanist Erasmus and the Swiss Reformer Zwingli. The Anabaptists in that century without exception concerned themselves with it, some more, some less. These are the people whose views and convictions I want to describe in the following chapters. I will also include in my descriptions several others who were part of what we call the Radical Reformation, but who were not Anabaptists.

All of these people confidently believed that they were living at the End of the Ages. They had no doubt of it. Some were impatient for the End to begin and among them were some who set about to get the schedule of events moving. Others, while certain of the nearness of the End, decided to wait quietly for its arrival. All of them strove with all their might to keep oil in their lamps and so to be ready when the Bridegroom would appear.

I. The Tapestry of Medieval Apocalyptic

"The most fundamental appeal of apocalypticism is the conviction it holds forth that time is related to eternity, that the history of man has a discernible structure and meaning in relation to its End, and that this End is the product not of chance, but of divine plan." So wrote Bernard McGinn in the introduction to his volume of sources for medieval apocalyptic.[1] Apocalyptic is therefore never a parlour game or an academic diversion. It has to do with living in the present in the light of a known past and a hoped-for future. The shape of any particular apocalyptic vision will reflect the religious and political specifics of contemporary experience. This is the way it was from the beginning of Christian history to the sixteenth century.

The major components of Christian apocalyptic thinking were derived from Judaism. This is demonstrable in all the major blocks of apocalyptic discourse in the New Testament, in the Gospels, in II Thessalonians 2, and in the Revelation of John. These were combined especially with the book of Daniel and IV Esdras and formed the apocalyptic corpus used henceforth.

The claim often made that apocalyptic expectation waned after the year 1000 has little basis in fact, for it is possible to trace an unbroken tradition of apocalyptic thought through the early centuries.[2] The first major writer was Irenaeus, bishop of Lyons in Gaul from ca. 180-200. His considerations of the end of history include discussions of the Antichrist and his identity, and an extensive description of the millennium. The fact that his work was written against the gnostics may account for his emphasis on a material millennium. Irenaeus was the first to identify the Antichrist as Jewish, coming from the tribe of Dan rather than from persecuting Rome. A more favourable view of the Roman Empire was developing among Christians at this time which may account for this shift away from identifying the Antichrist with Rome.[3] After

---

[1]McGinn 1979, 36.

[2]Ibid., 16, 14.

[3]Tertullian, writing in *Apology* 32 about the year 200 prayed for the Roman Empire's continuance, for it alone held back the coming of the Antichrist.

this the Jewish origin became standard in the biographies of the Antichrist in the Middle Ages.

It was Hippolytus of Rome who, about the year 200, wrote his *Commentary on Daniel*, which Bernard McGinn says is the "earliest complete Christian exegetical work" extant.[4] Hippolytus apparently wrote at a time of apocalyptic expectation because he was concerned to show by his calculations that the end was still some time in the future, no sooner than the year 500, for he calculated Jesus to have been born in the year 5500.[5] That meant that the sixth day of the world still had 500 years to go. The timetable of the end that was used right into Reformation times was already complete in Hippolytus' commentary. According to his calculations the fourth kingdom, the Roman, would be followed by the final week, the seven years of the endtime. In the first three and one half years the two witnesses Elijah and Enoch would preach, and in the remaining three and one half years the Antichrist would make war on the saints. At this point new details emerged. The Antichrist would first defeat Egypt, Libya, and Ethiopia,[6] and then proceed to draw all of mankind to him.[7] The destruction of the Antichrist would occur at Christ's return.[8] Hippolytus also collated the Daniel passages with related parts of the Revelation of John and other texts he considered relevant. The work on *Christ and Antichrist* is in fact a collation of all the passages Hippolytus considered pertinent to the subject.

The third major patristic writer of apocalyptic was Lactantius, writing between 304 and 313. The seventh book of his *Divine Institutes* provides a mass of detail regarding endtime events.[9] He clearly states that the end will come only with the demise of Rome, which, he states, will inevitably fall as all preceding empires have done.[10] The great enemy, the Antichrist, would come from the north.[11] This may well reflect the growing consciousness that the Empire's greatest threats came from the Germanic tribes north of the

[4]Ibid., 22.

[5]*Daniel II*, 3-7.

[6]*Christ and Antichrist*, 52.

[7]Ibid., 55-6.

[8]Ibid., 43-63; *Daniel II*, 39-40.

[9]McGinn 1979A, 25-80.

[10]*Divine Institutes*, VII, 15.

[11]Ibid., 16.

Danube and east of the Rhine. Actually Lactantius seems to provide for two Antichrists, the second to come from Syria.[12] When the Syrian Antichrist was destroyed the millennium would come, a time of peace and plenty.[13] Unique to Lactantius are his frequent references to classical writings and especially to the Sibyls, the female classical oracles who had been baptized into Christianity. These oracles, especially the Tiburtine and Cumaean Sibyls, became part of the authority for endtime events.[14] They appear in sixteenth century literature and were included among the Old Testament prophets by Michelangelo in his fresco on the ceiling of the Sistine Chapel. There are many other voices from patristic times and all testify to continuing concern with the events of the endtime.

Major changes in patristic thought were brought about by Constantine's conversion to Christianity. There was a reaction to the literal interpretation of Daniel and Revelation. Although Cyril of Jerusalem in the year 350 could still write in the earlier mode, a new interpretation of apocalyptic texts gradually asserted itself. As the Empire was christianized the influence of Alexandria with its allegorical method of scriptural interpretation made possible a reinterpretation. Eusebius of Caesarea, the court theologian of Constantine the Great, rejected literal apocalyptic expectations. In fact, it was he who gave most currency to the conviction that in the Christian empire "the kingdoms of this world had become the kingdom of the Lord and of his Christ." This note is barely concealed in the last chapter of his *Ecclesiastical History*,[15] and clearly stated in his *Oration*. Swords had been turned into ploughshares, fulfilling the prophetic word, and God's final peace enfolded the world.[16] Since the millennium had arrived, there was no need for any more apocalyptic speculation.

The man who did the most, however, to shape the mainline developments in eschatology in the church during the Middle Ages was Tyconius, a Donatist theologian, c. 330-390, about whom, for obvious reasons, we know very little. His commentary on the book of Revelation and in particular his hermeneutical method profoundly influenced Augustine. Tyconius regarded persecution of the

---

[12]Ibid., 17.

[13] Ibid., 24.

[14]Ibid., 16, 18, 19, 20, 23, 24, 25.

[15]*Ecclesiastical History*, X, 9.

[16]*Oration*, XVI, 3-8.

Donatist church as the "abomination of desolation."[17] But the fact that the persecution came from the Roman church and a "christian" emperor required an interpretation of the apocalyptic passages in the Bible that departed from the pre-Constantinian literal-historical interpretation.

Thus Tyconius resorted to a typological or symbolic approach. He viewed every symbol as working in two ways, positive and negative. The church which he considered to be one body also included the antichurch. It could therefore represent both Christ and Antichrist. Thus the church was composed of true believers and hypocrites, and the hypocrites were identical with the Antichrist collectively.[18] The Antichrist was therefore already in the world, primarily in the false prophets and priests in the church. These represented the tail of the dragon that swept away a third of the stars - Christians, who were attracted by the world away from the heaven of the church. This corporate Antichrist destroyed by means of his sacraments. Thus priests who were lovers of the world and whose god was their belly could not be guides to salvation. The true believer should therefore flee from the sacraments they administered. Whoever denied the incarnate Logos, that is, whoever hated his brother, belonged to the Antichrist. Hate and violence were the means by which the Antichrist established himself.[19] And although Tyconius evidently believed that the end was near because of the deteriorating conditions he saw around him, he completely rejected the literal-historical interpretation for a symbolic one. He was rescued for the church by Augustine who depended on Tyconius both for his eschatology and his interpretive method, a debt he did not hesitate to acknowledge.[20]

Augustine was fundamental to the "official" position of the medieval church regarding the apocalyptic texts. He worked with them in Book XX of the *City of God.* He assumed the scheme of the cosmic week, six days of history, and the seventh, the eternal Sabbath.[21] During the six ages, the great struggle between God and Satan would transpire. It would end in God's judgment. To that extent Augustine, as did all other Christian writers, assumed an historical process. But Augustine resolutely refused to give any literal value to the concepts of Antichrist, Gog and Magog, the millennium, and the Ten

---

[17] Rauh 1973, 105.

[18] Ibid., 107-109.

[19] Ibid., 11-115.

[20] Ibid., 119.

[21] *City of God* XX, 7; See Schmidt 1955, 288-318.

Kings. He took Christ's 1000-year reign of peace to be the present age, beginning with Christ's first appearance.[22] In any event, the number 1000 meant for him simply completeness. The Ten Kings of Daniel were not to be understood as literal kings but as a number denoting full sovereignty.[23] The sea of Revelation 20:13 simply meant the world.[24] The same approach was taken to identifying the meaning of the term "antichrist." Antichrist could be a person or a collective[25] (Augustine confessed ignorance on this point), but in whatever guise it appeared, Antichrist would always be overweening pride (superbia) that opposes God. As Tyconius had understood before him, Augustine believed the mystery of iniquity to be the constantly growing mass of hypocrites in the church and the heretics outside.[26] He resolutely rejected all calculation of endtime events as speculation and therefore useless.[27] The church, he said, was always persecuted, the Antichrist was always present, but Christ's reign of peace was also a present reality. This was known not so much on a map of the world and in history but on the map of the spiritual world of symbols and at the interface between time and eternity. There was no progress in Augustine's view of history; only the transpiring of the time God had allotted to the world.

Bernard McGinn and other scholars have shown that concern for the eschaton was continuous in the Western church[28], and that there was some continuity from one to the other in the most important apocalyptic texts from the Middle Ages. In these texts it is possible to distinguish two streams of interpretation - the literal-historical, taking its beginnings in the New Testament and the ante-Nicene Fathers, and the symbolic beginning with Tyconius and Augustine.

While, as already discussed above, a new kind of interpretation developed in the wake of the Emperor's conversion, the older literal-historical view continued as well. It experienced periodic revivals, usually at times of crisis.

---

[22]*City of God* XX, 7, 9.

[23]Ibid., 23.

[24]Ibid., 15.

[25]Ibid., 19. See also Rauh 1973, 122.

[26]Rauh 1973, 127.

[27]*City of God* XVIII, 52-53.

[28]McGinn 1979 and 1979A, and Staehelin 1951.

Such was the case at the time of the dissolution of the Empire in the West.[29] Apocalyptic concerns were alive in Byzantium as well.[30] Indeed, it was an apocalyptic document from Byzantium which McGinn calls "the crown of Eastern Christian apocalyptic literature" that now goes under the title *Pseudo-Methodius*, that did much to shape the specifics of apocalyptic speculation in the West.[31]

The context of this document was the Muslim conquests of the seventh century. Written soon after 660, it was a political pamphlet designed to keep alive the sense of belonging to the Byzantine Empire among those Syrian Christians who had come under Arab domination.[32] The Muslims were already identified as one of the great opponents of Christ in the endtime and this designation continued into the seventeenth century.[33] Included also in this work for the first time was the view of how the Last Emperor would take his place in the events of the endtime. How did this view emerge? The writer seems to have accepted the longstanding conviction that the Antichrist would make his appearance only after the Roman Empire had come to its end. But the idea that that Empire would be destroyed as had the three preceding empires was no longer tolerable. The simplest way of resolving it was to have the last emperor surrender it.[34]

When the Son of perdition has arisen, the king of the Romans will ascend Golgotha upon which the wood of the Holy Cross is fixed, in the place where the Lord underwent death for us. The king will take the crown from his head and place it on the Cross and stretching out his hands to heaven will hand over the kingdom of the Christians to God the Father . . . .When the Cross has been lifted up on high to heaven, the king of the Romans will directly give up his spirit. Then every principality and power will be destroyed that the Son of Perdition may be manifest . . . .[35]

[29]McGinn 1979, 51-5.

[30]Ibid., 56-61, 66-69.

[31]Ibid., 70. The basic Latin text published in Sackur 1898.

[32]Kmosko 1931, 291.

[33]McGinn 1979, 72.

[34]Ibid., 71.

[35]Ibid., 76.

This view became a standard feature of the apocalyptic landscape in the Middle Ages.[36] But whereas in *Pseudo-Methodius* the Emperor was clearly Byzantine, he became German or French when the story migrated to the West. We also encounter here several other items of interest. One is the use of the legend of Alexander the Great. According to Tacitus and others, including Jerome, Alexander had built a great gate in the Caucasus Mountains to shut in the Scythians. By the fifth century C.E. the Scythians were identified with the apocalyptic peoples of Gog and Magog and the apocalyptic connection had been made.[37] The legend was repeatedly modified in succeeding centuries to suit changing conditions. It was very influential because it promised victory over those nations which would eventually break through Alexander's Gate.[38]

One other feature of the *Pseudo-Methodius* is important. The Cross of Golgotha, on which the Last Emperor laid his crown, would together with the crown be taken up into heaven. "This is because the Cross on which our Lord Jesus Christ hung for the common salvation of all will begin to appear before him at his coming. . . ."[39] This is a reference to Matthew 24:30 and "the sign of the Son of Man." This belief too became a standard component in Western apocalyptic.

The figure of the Antichrist both corporate and personal continued to occupy the Western imagination.[40] About the year 950 Adso, Abbot of the cluniac abbey of Montier-en-Der northwest of Troyes, wrote a little treatise on the *Origin and Time of the Antichrist*. It came in the form of a letter to Gerberga, queen of the Frankish emperor Ludwig IV. It was a time of extreme violence and instability in the Empire. The breakdown following the partition of the Empire after Charlemagne had left people at the mercy of roving bands of pillaging and murdering warriors. Outside invasion from Magyars, Norsemen, and Muslims was a daily possibility.[41] No wonder, then, that people believed that the end was near. Gerberga had requested clarification about the end, and Adso produced it. The figure of the Antichrist here is that of an historical individual. The document purports to be a biography constructed from Scripture and its interpreters. The Antichrist was born in

[36]See Zeschwitz 1881.

[37]Anderson 1932.

[38]McGinn 1979, 72.

[39]Ibid., 76.

[40]See Konrad 1964, 54-70.

[41]McGinn 1979A, 83.

Babylon of the tribe of Dan, raised in the towns of Bethsaida and Chorazin. He emerged as the great deceiver after he had killed the two witnesses Elijah and Enoch. He would deceive the Jews with his claims to be the Messiah and would enthrone himself in the church as well. There would be a terrible tribulation in which he would try to turn everyone away from God. But on the Mount of Olives he would be slain by the power of Christ.[42]

Several special features in this account deserve mention. The first is the adaptation of the legend of the Last Emperor to Western realities. The old empire is in ruins, wrote Adso, but the kings of the Franks now possess it; thus the last emperor will be a king of the Franks.[43] Another feature was the deliberate opposing of the Antichrist to Christ at every point in his life and career. The following words are clearly modelled on Colossians 2:9. "The fullness of diabolical power and of the whole character of evil will dwell in him in bodily fashion; for in him will be hidden all the treasures of malice and iniquity."[44] A third feature is that the Antichrist would take his seat in the temple of God. At one point the author identified that seat with a rebuilt temple in Jerusalem, but at another point he identified it as "Holy Church."[45] Thus, the view of the Antichrist being at the heart of the church was preserved even in the literalist tradition of interpretation.

The other thread, that of the symbolic interpretation of apocalyptic Scriptures was not lost in the revival of the literal interpretation. The tradition of Tyconius was carried forward, for instance, in the commentary on the book of Revelation by the Spanish monk Beatus of Liebana in the middle of the eighth century.[46] But in the eleventh and twelfth centuries we meet the most sophisticated interpreters in the Tyconian tradition in the persons of Gerhoh von Reichersberg and Otto von Freising, both of them highly educated churchmen, both of them bishops. They wrote in the context of the great struggle between emperor and pope over the control of the church. Both saw the work of the Antichrist in the schism, Gerhoh specifically identifying Emperor Henry IV as a tool of Satan. But beyond this kind of general reference Gerhoh rejected the literal interpretation. He said that there was no evidence for the view that the Antichrist came from the tribe of Dan. For him

---

[42]Ibid, 90-96. McGinn's translation is based on the critical Latin text of Verhelst 1976.

[43]Ibid., 93.

[44]Ibid.

[45]Ibid., 91, 94.

[46]McGinn 1979, 77-79.

Babylon was a symbol for the world and the Temple for the church.[47] The Antichrist had in fact been at work in the world since the beginning and was identified especially by his persecution of the church in four periods, the last of which would come through the avarice of the Curia now that the Church had become a great power. There were false brethren and hypocrites who made the situation especially dangerous.[48]

Otto von Freising wrote a world history with the title *Chronica sive historia duabus civitatibus* (Chronicle of the History of the Two Cities).[49] Otto was the most famous of the symbolists and noted for his view of history. His discussion of eschatology in the last book of his *Chronicle* is not a postscript. It belongs integrally to the whole work. He believed that history is what takes place on earth between creation and judgment. The whole course of that history was known because it was limited.[50] Although the events still to transpire have not yet happened, they are known in broad outline through revelation. God himself is in charge; man is not autonomous, but an instrument in God's hands.[51]

Augustine and Orosius were Ottos's models.[52] Thus he tells a story of two cities which have always existed in the world side by side. The city of God began small and gradually grew larger. In the future it alone will be established by God in full perfection. The city of earth, on the other hand, dominated at the beginning, but in reverse order is ineluctably moving towards its destruction.[53] The city of God is the *civitas permixta* as in Augustine, especially in the period following the conversion of Constantine. Still, in it the kingdom of Christ reached the perfection that is possible on earth.[54] City of God and Church are therefore one and the same thing.[55]

[47]Rauh 1973, 450-1; Meuthen 1959, 143-4.

[48]McGinn 1979, 104-7; Rauh 1973, 468-9.

[49]Lammers 1974.

[50]Ibid., XLII.

[51]Ibid., IV, 2; III, Introduction.

[52]Ibid., I, Introduction; VIII, Introduction.

[53]Ibid.

[54]Ibid., VI, 36.

[55]Ibid., VIII, Introduction.

Otto also used a system of time periods and ages. Basically there were three ages. The first was from the beginning to the conversion of Constantine; the second from Constantine to Otto's own time, the time of the great struggle; the third was the time of perfection after the Judgment. The history of the city of earth also had a tripartite division. The first was the time before grace, that is, from the beginning to the time of Christ; the second was from Christ until the Judgment; the third was the eternal retribution. The city of God moved from lesser to greater perfection; the city of earth from lesser to greater destruction.[56]

Otto also worked with the cosmic week but nowhere discusses it in particular.[57] It does, however, emerge from the division of the work itself into eight books: the seven days of the cosmic week, plus the great eighth day of eternity.

He also addressed the old scheme of the four kingdoms, with Rome as the last.[58] However, like Augustine, he was very ambivalent about Rome. On the one hand the city of God had come to its greatest fulfilment under this empire. On the other, it was destined to sink into destruction as had all the others.[59] In Otto's view, in contrast to earlier views, the actual empire of Rome, therefore, did not have the function of restraining the Antichrist. Nor did Otto resort to the Last Emperor as a solution to this problem. Rather, he identified the monastic orders as the power that restrained the Antichrist.[60] Otto positioned his "hymnic account" of the monks in the very last chapter of Book VII. "They remain untouched by the . . . catastrophes of the course of this world," he wrote, "and, after six days of toil, they enjoy a foretaste of eternal rest in the peace of the true Sabbath . . . ."[61] They were the high point of the gradual unveiling of the city of God. From this point on Otto could discuss only the ultimate events of the Antichrist, resurrection, judgment, and the blessedness of the eighth day.

[56]Ibid.

[57]Ibid., II, Introduction; VIII, 13, 34.

[58]Ibid., Letter to Rainald von Dassel; II, 13; III, Introduction; VIII, 14.

[59]Ibid., III, Introduction.

[60]Ibid., VII, 21, 35.

[61]Ibid., VII, 35.

Otto's *Chronica* is a very large work and much has been omitted in this brief sketch.[62] However, one more issue - Otto's symbolism - needs to be mentioned briefly. For one thing, like earlier symbolists, Otto did not make any specific identification of who the Antichrist might be, but identified his activities broadly with what began to happen in the church in the great struggle between Empire and Papacy in the eleventh century.[63] His work could also be seen in the church in the activities of the heretics and hypocrites.[64]

History was not seen by Otto as cause and effect in the sense that one event was immediately the cause of the following one. Rather he saw the relationships in terms of types and their recurrence. The threefold triumph for Augustus as supreme ruler on 6 January after the conclusion of the civil war was prophetic of the visit of the three magi in Bethlehem, establishing Jesus as king of kings.[65] There were ten persecutions from Nero to Constantine. As Pharaoh was destroyed when he attempted an eleventh persecution, so the city of earth would initiate an eleventh and last persecution under its head the Antichrist, at the end of which the people with him would be completely destroyed.[66] This view was possible because of the conviction already referred to that God is in control of the process. By means of such figures and types it was possible to see order and coherence in history, and by means of them it was possible to make shrewd extrapolations for the future as well.

Although Otto refrained from identifying anyone as the Antichrist, and assigned symbolic value to much of Christian eschatology,[67] he was convinced that the end was near.[68] This conviction underlay the arrangement of his materials. Much of the legacy of Otto von Freising is found again in the writings of his fellow-Cistercian Joachim of Fiore.

Joachim is the single most important figure in medieval apocalyptic. Much has been written about him during this century,[69] but no complete

---

[62]See Spörl 1965 and Koch 1965.

[63]Ibid., VI, 35-36. See also Rauh 1973, 314ff.

[64]Ibid., II, 22; IV, 5.

[65]Ibid., III, 6.

[66]Ibid., III, 45.

[67]See especially his discussion of eschatological particulars in Book VIII.

[68]Ibid., II, 13, V, Introduction.

[69]See McGinn 1975 and Reeves 1976.

translation of his works exists,[70] although the main Latin works have been photographically reprinted in our time.[71] Joachim was a man of astonishing imaginative powers who, without intending it, produced an unparalleled crop of apocalyptic writing and acting. He had the reputation of a prophet in his lifetime and was regularly appealed to into the seventeenth century.[72]

His prophetic understanding began about the year 1183 and stemmed from a vision he had in which he suddenly saw with great clarity the relationships of the two biblical Testaments to each other.[73] This happened on Easter morning. Joachim also describes a second illumination which took place on the day of Pentecost in which he suddenly understood the mystery of the Holy Trinity.[74] As a result of these visions the Bible became his sole source for developing his theory of history, and the doctrine of the Trinity provided the main structure for it. In both accounts Joachim confessed that he had been struggling to get clarity. There was an urgency to know spurred by contemporary events. The conflict between Church and Empire, which had begun over a century earlier, had not been resolved. A resurgence of Islam was taking place which in 1187, four years after the Easter vision, led to the fall of Jerusalem. Two of Joachim's letters that have survived testify to his conviction that the end of all things was very near, within a generation.[75]

Joachim's understanding of the relationship of the Testaments was expressed in his famous trinitarian scheme of the three ages, the ages of the Father, Son, and Holy Spirit. The first age began with Adam, the second with King Uzziah, the third with Benedict of Nursia.[76] These ages were identified not by a scheme of years but of human generations. However, the three ages overlapped. Not only did the first and second, and second and third overlap, but also the first and the third. Fortunately, Joachim or someone close to him,

---

[70]Translations of selected parts in McGinn 1979, 130-141; McGinn 1979A, 113-48; and some portions in German in Rosenberg 1955, 66-148.

[71]*Concordia* 1519, *Expositio* 1527, *Psalterium* 1527. Modern editions of some works have been published. See Burger 1986, page 97 for a list of ancient and modern editions of Joachim's works.

[72]Reeves 1976, chapter 6.

[73]*Expositio* f. 39a-b; McGinn 1979, 130.

[74]*Psalterium* f.227a; Rosenberg 1955, 73-4.

[75]McGinn 1979A, 113-19.

[76]*Expositio* f.5a-b; McGinn 1979, 133-4. *Concordia* f.82b; McGinn 1979A, 123-4.

supplied us with a series of diagrams which visualize what he had in mind.[77] The one diagram which is perhaps most useful here is the figure of the three trinitarian circles.[78] The first age was that of the law, the second that of the Gospel, and the third the time of spiritual understanding. He used triplets to aid in understanding the differences between the ages: knowledge, wisdom, complete understanding; servitude of slaves, service of sons, complete freedom; plagues, action, contemplation; fear, faith, love; starlight, dawn, full daylight; nettles, roses, lilies; water, wine, oil.[79] All of them proclaim progression from lesser to greater integration.

It was the Third Age, of course, that caught the attention of Joachim's contemporaries and followers. It was to be the time of the Spirit, a time when God would no longer reveal himself as before in literal and historical fashion. In fact in the Third Age men would flee from these earlier forms of revelation. Even mystical images and metaphors would disappear, and men would see the countenance of God in the Spirit because they would have become like him.[80]

Joachim envisaged a community that would be the carrier of the new spiritual knowledge, the spiritual men (viri spirituales).[81] This new community would be one that included monks, clergy, and laity, all under the leadership of an angelic pope.[82] It is also clear that there would be people outside this community so that even in the full flowering of the Third Age, which Joachim expected to come about the year 1260, there would be growth. In Joachim's time the monastic communities were understood by themselves and others to be the ideal divine community. In Joachim's new community, clergy and laity were included.

However, even there the monks were at the top. In fact, two new orders would emerge who would be the preachers of the gospel in word and deed until the end. One of them would "gather in the harvest of evil in the spirit of Elijah."[83] This is the first reference in Christian apocalyptic literature to a

---

[77]Reeves and Hirsch-Reich 1972.

[78]McGinn 1979A, 105. The circles

[79]*Concordia* f.112a; Rosenberg 1955, 82-3.

[80]Rosenberg 1955, 118.

[81]McGinn 1979A, 143.

[82]Ibid., 142-48; *Concordia* f.56a; McGinn 1979, 134-5.

[83]*Expositio* f.175b-176a; McGinn 1979, 136-7.

specific elect group of spirit-filled believers as the executors of God's wrath on the godless.

While the three ages dominated as the main scheme of history, Joachim also used the cosmic week scheme of earlier interpreters. It was, as it were, superimposed on the three ages. The first six ages came to an end in the work of John the Baptist. The seventh age, which was Saturday, extended over the whole age of the Spirit. All of that was part of the course of history on this earth. The eighth day, Sunday, was the blessedness of saints and martyrs with the Triune God in heaven.[84]

We cannot leave Joachim without commenting on his views regarding Elijah and the Antichrist. The figure of Elijah was part of the apocalyptic furniture of every interpreter. Joachim wrote that Elijah belonged to the Third Age even as Moses belonged to the second.   That was so because Elijah was the prototype of the ideal monk, a thoroughly spiritual man, celibate, leading a lonesome and separated life.[85] Elijah would be revealed again at the end. He would inaugurate the Third Age and was a symbol of the Holy Spirit.[86]

In his notes on the figure of the seven-headed dragon, Joachim identified the seven heads as seven persecutions. The sixth one under Saladin had begun, and the seventh would follow. The king of the seventh persecution was called the Antichrist, but another, Gog, was to be the real Antichrist. The first would come secretly, the second openly. The king called Antichrist would come from the West and initiate a tribulation which would last forty-two months. After that there would be a time of peace and justice of unknown length. Then Satan would again be unleashed and then that other Antichrist, signified by the tail of the dragon, would appear. He and his host would be destroyed by God.[87] Joachim too believed that the Roman Empire held back the Antichrist,[88] but there is in his writing nothing about the Last World Emperor who would surrender the sovereignty.

Joachim rejected the Augustinian static view of history and saw movement and progression towards a time when God's will would be done on earth. He

[84]Rosenberg 1955, 99-103.

[85]Rosenberg 1955, 97.

[86]Reeves and Hirsch-Reich 1972, 196-7.

[87]McGinn 1979A, 136-40.

[88]*Expositio* f.134a-b.

combined in his writings a typological and symbolic exegesis with a view of history on the move. To be sure, that history was an expression of the very being of the trinitarian God, and could not benefit from human initiative. Joachim had no vision of overturning the Church and the Empire. Still, as Bernard McGinn wrote:

> Joachim's stress on the domination of the spiritual and charismatic over the institutional and rational in the future church was diametrically opposed to the forces that triumphed in the thirteenth century. . . . In this sense the concept of the third age . . . was a radical critique of the thirteenth century church.[89]

This critique bore rich if sometimes destructive fruit in succeeding centuries.

The volume of apocalyptic writing increased steadily in the next three centuries. Joachim had released into European society certain ideas that became vehicles for frustrations and dissatisfactions and hostility toward existing institutions. He died in 1202. In 1215 the Fourth Lateran Council condemned Joachim's attack upon Peter Lombard's trinitarian theology. This act immediately put all of Joachim's work in an official shadow, particularly since his trinitarian views were so fundamental to his view of history and especially of the Third Age. According to McGinn, Joachim's attack marks the beginning of the reaction against the Papacy,[90] which was to lead ultimately to its identification with the Antichrist. One of the first traces of this is found in the exchange of calumnies that characterized the struggle between Frederick II and the Papacy. One of Frederick's supporters identified Innocent IV as the Antichrist by showing that his name represented the number 666.[91]

At this time all the apocalyptic themes of earlier centuries were commented upon and expanded, not only by clergy as heretofore, but also by lay people. Joachim's florid and enticing numerology[92] gave rise to new computations. The Franciscan General Bonaventure expressed his convictions on the subject in sermons delivered in Paris a year before his death. Although profoundly influenced by Joachim, he went back to the six ages scheme. He

---

[89]McGinn 1979, 129.

[90]Ibid., 159.

[91]Ibid., 175-6; McGinn 1978, 155-173.

[92]*Concordia* f.56a; f.31b; f.105b-106a; f.22a.

believed the sixth age was nearly over because Francis of Assisi had been identified with the Angel of the Sixth Seal, and as the promise of the new order of the seventh age.[93] The Spiritual Franciscans Olivi and Ubertino of Casale also gave attention to this, modifying earlier interpretation to fit new times.[94]

The Avignonese exile of the church and the Great Schism gave rise to a sense of the approaching end as much as the struggle between Empire and Church had done two centuries earlier. As Marjorie Reeves wrote: "The Great Schism brought into sharpest possible focus all the various elements of the prophetic tradition . . .:the forces of the Antichrist creating schism and persecution in the Church, the expectation of terrible tribulations and judgments."[95] So despairing were the people of that time of the ability of the church to reform itself, that the old prophecy of the Last Emperor was revived again. This time the Last Emperor's main role was to be the reformer of the church.[96] Telesphorus of Cosenza, a monk, constructed a whole new chronology to deal with these shattering events, including angelic popes, antichristian emperors , and several Antichrists.[97] The great conciliator professor Pierre D'Ailly, himself from that bastion of scholasticism, the University of Paris, expressed the view that this might be the great schism that would precede the coming of the Antichrist.[98] Nicholas of Cusa, the greatest intellect of the fifteenth century, also developed a chronology for the appearance of the Antichrist.[99]

A striking figure in this setting was the Dominican Vincent Ferrer, who preached in the opening years of the fifteenth century. He was convinced that the Schism of the Church was the harbinger of the Antichrist and he travelled up and down Europe with his message. His method was to cite the words of earlier prophets.[100] A final nameless prophet wrote an enigmatic prophecy at the beginning of the Schism that begins with the words: "In that day the

---

[93]McGinn 1979, 197-202.

[94]Ibid., 208-212.

[95]Reeves 1969, 422.

[96]McGinn 1979, 350-1; *Sigismundi*, f.diia-diiia.

[97]McGinn 1979, 249-50.

[98]Reeves 1969, 422.

[99]McGinn 1979, 255.

[100]Ibid., 256-8.

eagle will come. . .," apparently a reference to a destroying king who, together with an illegitimate pope, was to be defeated to make room for a time of peace and justice.[101] The eagle was a prevalent polyvalent symbol of apocalyptic literature from Daniel to Revelation.

Joachim's prophecy of the coming order of spiritual men produced a great harvest. The Franciscans first claimed to be its fulfilment and the Dominicans were not far behind.[102] Later the Spirituals understood themselves to be the seraphic order and soon other groups also began to see themselves in that light. The last group to claim the distinction was Loyola's Society of Jesus.

Joachim had made much of the fact that the spiritual men would be taught directly by God and would in fact flee from what was then regarded as knowledge. This note began to increase in volume, in considerable part because popular prophetism was profoundly anticlerical. It led ultimately to the conclusion that when simple people began to speak for themselves and provide their own answers to the questions of faith, the endtime had arrived.

This summary indicates that there was an unbroken tradition of apocalyptic thought in Western Christianity from the beginning to the sixteenth century. It is immensely rich in images, in its understanding of Scripture, and in the variety of themes. There is a distinction between literal and symbolic interpretations up to Joachim. Following Joachim the literal and the symbolic were usually mixed, but a popular stream emerged alongside the official one. The official version of apocalyptic thought tended always to symbolic interpretations. The Augustinian view of history as static was admirably suited to the powerful bureaucratic church, intent on preserving and strengthening its position. The veiled Joachimite critique of that church, by giving prominence to a future spiritual church, was virtually fated in the following centuries to produce antichurch and anticlerical postures. Apocalyptic was by no means the preserve only of the poor and dispossessed. The powerful used it to bolster their positions and to maintain things as they were. Ordinary people used apocalyptic to strike out in new directions whenever they came to believe that things did not need to continue as they were.

[101]Ibid., 255-6.

[102]Reeves 1969, 422.

II. The Last Age of the World

1. "These last and perilous times"

The sixteenth century was, like our own, a time of upheaval and overthrow. "The ever whirling wheels of Change" seemed to spin ever faster. And while the change and the break with much of the past were greeted with loud applause, they were also the occasion of anxiety and foreboding. Both the applause for the long-awaited changes and the anxious brooding over the precariousness of an uncertain future were fed by Europe's authors and publishers. Booklets and pamphlets written by what were then called the "new evangelicals", the followers of Martin Luther and Huldrych Zwingli, announced the downfall of the great papal church that had dominated Europe for so long. But what would be put in its place was far from clear in 1525. The writers of the church of Rome denounced the "new evangelicals" as heretics and enemies of God, but it was clear to them as to everyone else that things could never again be as they had been. It has been estimated that one booklet addressing itself to the pressing issues of the time was printed for every man, woman, and child in German-speaking Europe in the 1520s (Kohler 1987, 337). This is an amazing fact when one considers that between 90 and 95% of the population could neither read nor write. Those who could became the transmitters of the new ideas to those who could not.

Among the thousands of *Flugschriften* published in those years were many on the subject of the endtimes. They were astrological predictions, compilations of the ancient prophecies of Methodius, St. Bridget, Joachim of Fiore, and the Merlin of the King Arthur legends. There were selected oracles of the Sibyls, the pagan female counterparts of the male Hebrew prophets. There were books dealing with contemporary prodigies, eclipses, planetary conjunctions, and comets, all omens of disaster. There were the illustrated books about the ancestry and history of the Antichrist and of the 15 signs that were to usher in the End (Das Puch von dem Entkrist). There were publications which identified the Pope as the Antichrist and Luther as Elijah returned or as the great angel of the Apocalypse. These books were read aloud in taverns, houses, and on village greens, and they filled the imagination of noble, intellectual, and commoner alike with events so large and powerful that mountains and rivers, and even planets and stars would be moved out of their courses. How could mere mortals survive such terrors? The Anabaptists, beginning with 1525, were part of that world. We should not imagine them as being withdrawn and separate from the rest of the world, but rather as right in the middle of it. They contributed significantly to the general endtime expectation, through their own writings and also, in the view of Protestants and Catholics, as a sign of the great wickedness and apostasy of the last times.

During the whole of the sixteenth century and on into the seventeenth people were certain that they were living at the extreme edge of time. It was like the experience of expecting a storm or a tornado in the late afternoon of a very hot day. We all know the signs; a gradually darkening sky, a great stillness, lightening flashes, growling thunder in the distance. We fasten things down and prepare to take shelter. Everyone in the community can see it coming. There is a consensus concerning the coming storm. In the 1500s people spoke and wrote about living in "these last and perilous times."[1] Political, religious, and social conditions and events menaced and threatened. Strife was everywhere and exploitation and the pursuit of wealth, and those whose calling it was to be examples to the faithful were afflicted with the worst vices. It seemed that the measure of wickedness was full. The end could therefore not be far away.[2] Michael Sattler saw the imminent destruction of the monster that was persecuting the church,[3] and the letters of Jacob Hutter reveal a growing sense of the approaching end amidst a crescendo of persecution and point forward to the marvelous reward God will give to the faithful.[4] Conrad Grebel was reported to have said that the Messiah was at the door.[5] This same expectation led Niklaus Guldi of St. Gall to urge his sisters

---

[1] Representative examples are: *QGTS* I, 31; Hubmaier, 72, 167; *GZ* I, 93; *QGW* II, 115, 26; *WPM*, 74, 104, 164, 371; *CS* I, 127; IX, 898, 901-04; *Hut. Ep.* I, 100, 217, 219; *QGTS* II, 471-2.

[2] Hubmaier, 114; *TA Hesse* 26, 53; *Judas*, Bib; *QGT* V, 71; *CWMS*, 1052; Verheus 1971, 87.

[3] Sattler, 56

[4] Hutter, 1979.

[5] *QGTS* I, 122.

and brothers to repent, for the axe was already laid to the tree.[6] In 1530 Martin Luther rushed his translation of the book of Daniel to the printers so that it would have a chance to warn people of the coming End. He was afraid he would not get his translation of the Bible finished before the Second Advent.[7] Two years later in 1532 Melchior Hoffman wrote that the fifth angel (Rev. 16:10) had already completed his task and that the two remaining angels were already set to pour out their bowls of God's wrath.[8] What can one conclude about the time, said Endres Keller in his interrogation in 1536, when a child, which is still too young to pray, already blasphemes God? Only that the time is short, for this is the desolating sacrilege of which Daniel prophesied (9:26). A Hessian Anabaptist reported in 1530 that they had been sure the end would come by St. Michael's Day (29 Sept.), or St. Martin's Day (11 Nov.), but that since those days had come and gone they could not imagine that the world could go on past Christmas.[9] Menno Simons, writing in 1539, gave voice to the continuing expectation of an early end of all things:

> Alas, it is about time to awake! Remember that the angel of Revelation has sworn by the eternal and living God . . . that after this time, there shall be time no more. From the Scriptures we cannot conclude but that this is the last festival of the year, the last proclamation of the holy Gospel, the last invitation to the marriage of the Lamb, which is to be celebrated, published, and sanctified before the great and terrible day of the Lord. With it, it seems, the summer will pass away and the winter come forth.[10]

The briefness of the time left makes it imperative to be watchful, not in order to avoid suffering, but in order to be able to identify the deceivers whose coming has been predicted for the Last Days. The deceivers are the clergy and the doctors who by stealth and trickery confuse the Gospel.[11] An anonymous Anabaptist apocalyptic tract of 1528 sees the devil roving abroad with his false teachings fronted by professors and clergy to seduce and confuse even the faithful if possible. His errors are so powerful that, if the Lord had not shortened the time, not a single soul would be saved.[12] It is a theme to which

---

[6]Ibid., 118.

[7]Torrance 1953, 43.

[8]*Zeucknus*, 432.

[9]*TA Hesse*, 25. See also *QGTS* II, 616, 622; *QGTÖ* I, 44; Wappler, 234, 259, 282.

[10]*O.O.*, 6; *CWMS*, 109.

[11]Preuss 1933, 98, 153.

[12]*Sendbrieff 1528*, D2b.

Melchior Hoffman returned repeatedly. The table of the Lord, he wrote, has become a snare for very many. Even the most intelligent and educated neither know Christ nor truly possess him. Instead, the mountain in which all true treasures are hidden is quite unknown to them. In them the old adage is fulfilled: "The more college, the less knowledge" (Je gelehrter, je verkehrter).[13] In 1544 Caspar Schwenckfeld made the same point. The deception even of Christians by which they were turned from the living, reigning Christ to the Antichrist, from a spiritual to a legalistic faith, was virtually complete. Hence the End could not be far off.[14]

2. Signs of the End

But there were much more specific indications that the End was near. Although every spokesman and writer in the 16th century reminded his readers that according to Scripture no one knew the exact day or hour of the End, nevertheless Jesus himself had told his disciples of signs to watch for by which one could at least attempt to establish the month or year.[15] Hence every interpreter enumerated the signs which pointed unerringly to the nearness of the End. Michael Servetus listed no fewer than 60 signs of the nearness of the End in his *Restitution*.[16] Most lists were shorter. Martin Luther drew attention to the general fear in which everyone lived in the 1520s. In one list he identified as specific signs the general moral decay, the repression and persecution of Christians, the constant universal warfare, the recurring plagues, the degeneration of nature, the new preaching of the Gospel,[17] and the 1522 prodigy of the "monk's calf" which he described in detail in a tract of 1523.[18] He also believed that the prevalence and spread of syphilis was a sign of the End.[19] Planetary conjunctions, eclipses, natural disasters and famine were more signs of the approaching End.[20] While he kept insisting that all of these have happened all through human history, they are signs of the End because

---

[13]*Majestat*, A1b; *Romeren*, A1b. Another translation might be: "The higher the degree, the further at sea."

[14]*CS* IX, 208.

[15]Daniel XII, F2a.

[16]Friedman 1978, 41.

[17]Preuss 1933, 96, 235-6.

[18]*Bapstesel 1523*, B1a.

[19]*Chronica*, O4a.

[20]*Adventspostille*, 104-5, 107-8.

they are now all coming together.[21]   These same signs are encountered again and again in the writings of the Radical Reformation.   Jacob Hutter wrote in a letter of 1535 about the unbridled godlessness and villainy of the time, the coldness of Christian love, the many false prophets and antichrists, the great shedding of blood, and the "abomination that desolates."[22]   Also considered as a sign by many was the expected early conversion of the Jews to Christ. Luther expected it to happen, and Melchior Hoffman saw it as inevitable for it was part of the package of endtime events.[23]   Writing in 1545 Caspar Schwenckfeld pointed to the Schmalcald War of that year as a sign of the End and also to the revealing of the Antichrist especially in the perversion of the Lord's Supper.[24]   In 1527 Andreas Osiander, the Lutheran reformer of Nuremberg, wrote a preface to an old prophecy attributed to Hildegard von Bingen (d. 1179) regarding the papacy.   In it he wrote that even though the papists had all the prophets, gospels, and epistles which tell them about the End, and also have the prophecies of their own bishops, monks and nuns, and of the astrologers, as well as the signs in the sky, they pay no attention.   Hence they will be overtaken by a disaster guided their way by God.[25]   Jacob Hutter also notes this phenomenon.   "Many people say," he wrote, "Time passes and every vision comes to nothing.   As the days pass, many scoffers say, Where is the promise of His Coming?   Everything is the same as it has always been. That is what . . . the Apostle Peter foretold.   These scoffers deliberately refuse to listen."[26]   The signs were there for everyone to see.   They were a mark of God's graciousness, giving to all every opportunity for repentance and salvation.   When the End would inevitably come, no one would have any excuse.

3.   Times and Chronologies

In his work *The Most Revealing Book of the Bible*, Vernard Eller calls those who do the endtime calculations calendarizers.   The calendarizers treat the Bible like a box of jigsaw puzzle pieces.   They take the pieces out one by one and gradually fit them into a picture.   But they do one thing no jigsaw enthusiast ever does; they take the freedom to create pieces of their own

---

[21]Ibid., 108.

[22]Hutter 1979, 94.

[23]*Romeren*, S1a.

[24]*CS* IX, 497-9.

[25]Osiander, *Hildegarde*, A2b.

[26]Hutter 1979, 94.   Cf. Franck, *Chronica* II, zz2a.

wherever there are gaps, or they commit the smaller sin of trimming existing pieces to fit the pattern that emerges. Thus the Bible functions quite simply as a container of scattered bits of oracular information, all equally inspired, which the prophetic interpreter gathers and fits into a calendar of events.

The twentieth century has no monopoloy on calendarizers. The Hal Lindseys have many, many ancestors, and they could save themselves a great deal of work while reaping the same profit if they simply used the work their ancestors did. All they have to do is fill in the blanks. They could use, for example, the solid work of Sts. Jerome or Augustine. There is the incredibly detailed, biblically eloquent Joachim of Fiore or one of his interpreters, Peter John Olivi. We have the anonymous writer of a fifteenth century theological textbook often quoted in the sixteenth century, or even the great Martin Luther himself. And if they want for something more complete and imaginative in the style of Joachim, they could work their way through the Anabaptist Melchior Hoffman's commentaries on Daniel and Revelation. The following is a short guide through the work of some of the calendarizers of the Radical Reformation. Careful attention must be given to that non-Anabaptist Martin Luther lest the reader think that the calendarizers are to be found only among the sects of Christendom.

For a man who, as he repeatedly said, regarded endtime chronologies with tolerant amusement, Luther himself made not a few attempts at calendarizing. In his introduction to this translation of Daniel he identified the four beasts of chapter 7 with the four kingdoms of Assyria/Babylon, Persia/Media, Greece, and Rome. The last had now broken up into ten kingdoms which were Syria, Egypt, Asia, Greece, Africa, Spain, France, Italy, Germany, and England. (He had to fudge a little there because Asia and Africa were scarcely kingdoms like France or England, but then that is permitted prophetic license.) The small horn of Daniel 7:8 he identified with the Turk who had now destroyed three of the ten, namely Egypt, Asia, and Greece. That meant, he concluded, that the Last Day had nearly arrived since, essentially, no biblical history remained.[27]

The tradition of dividing human history into six ages of a 1000 years each was transmitted to the Middle Ages by Augustine.[28] It became one of the standard schemes for comprehending world history, perhaps because of its

[27]*WA DB* 11/2, 12.

[28]*De Civitate Dei* II, 15-19.

simplicity. Luther used it in his chronology of world history first published in 1541.[29] He, however, acknowledged that he got it from a work of bishop Paul of Burgos (d. 1435), who in turn claimed to have gotten it from the Talmud.[30] This was called the prophecy of Elijah which said that the world would exist for 6000 years; 2000 years void, or formless (inane history), 2000 years of the Law, and 2000 years of Christ. Luther defended this by appealing to Psalm 90:4 and 2 Peter 3:8. After the six ages would follow the eternal Sabbath. He accepted the view that the birth of Jesus had taken place in the year 3960 after the creation.[31] Luther concluded that only a very short time was left, and that, since all the signs were there, the world could not possibly last until the year 2000. To get more precision he employed the biblical three and one half years, multiplied that by the 30 earthly years of Jesus, and got 105 years. Add those 105 years to 1453, the year of the fall of Constantinople and the beginning of the Turkish threat, and one got 1558 as the year of the End.[32] This may sound tongue-in-cheek, and Luther always said that such calculations could never be precise.[33] But one cannot avoid the conclusion that, beyond his occasional joking about it, he was serious. To conclude Luther's views, it is important to underscore that the most prominent man of the age concerned himself in detail with the events and the date of the End. In fact, he hoped and longed for it to come. Certainly his commitment to these matters legitimized such concern and activity also for others.

Given Luther's early interest in the events of the End as well as the work of people like almanac-writer Johann Carion, the astrologer Johannes Lichtenberger, and the cabalist Michael Stiefel, it is not surprising that Anabaptists and others close to them talked the same language from the beginning.[34]

The earliest Anabaptists in Zürich had a sense of the impending End, which increased to certainty of its immediacy in Michael Sattler's letter to the Anabaptists at Horb. There was no timetable left.

[29]Luther, *Chronica* 1559, B8b.

[30]Pflantz 1939, 37. Sanhedrin 97a and Aboda Sara 9a.

[31]Köstlin 1878, 132.

[32]Hillerdal 1954, 115.

[33]*Chronica*, A8a-B7b.

[34]See Klaassen 1985 and 1986.

The abomination of desolation is visible among you. The elect servants and maidservants of God will be marked on the forehead with the name of their Father. The world has risen up against those who are redeemed from its error. The gospel is testified to before all the world for a testimony. According to this the day of the Lord must no longer tarry.[35]

The first Anabaptist to establish a date for the end was Hans Hut, the fiery evangelist follower of Thomas Müntzer in 1527. From his own statements and those of his followers describing his views, the following chronology emerges. Identifying the beginning of the last seven years as 1521, perhaps with the work of the Zwickau Prophets, and the last three and a half with the Peasant Revolt and especially the work of Thomas Müntzer and his co-worker Heinrich Pfeiffer, Hut arrived at Pentecost, 1528, as the date of the End. He regarded Müntzer and Pfeiffer as the two witnesses of Revelation 11 whose bodies had literally not been buried after their execution. In the spring of 1527 the Turks would come, thus beginning God's judgment on the world, followed by plague, famine, war, and natural disasters. At this point, the end of the second three and a half years, Christ would come and give the sword to his elect, that is, all those marked with the sign of baptism on the forehead, and they would then exterminate the godless with the sword. After that would follow the Last judgment and the reign of the elect.[36]

A somewhat independent follower of Hut was Leonhard Schiemer, a former Franciscan, who was arrested as an Anabaptist leader late 1527. While in prison in Rattenberg, Tyrol, he wrote several tracts and letters. In his tract on the Twelve Articles of Christian Faith he gave his own calendar of the events of the End. He interpreted the number of the Antichrist, 666, not as six hundred and sixty six, but as three successive sixes, referring to the six ages of world history in which the Adversary has sought to confine everyone so that they won't come to the complete obedience of the seventh day.[37] In his detailed discussion of the endtime chronology he followed Hut's basic scheme which began in 1521 and was to end at Pentecost, 1528. The first three and one half years were the time during which the divine covenant was offered to people. Here he gives no details since all of that is past anyway, but goes on to the second three and one half years. The beginning of this period is marked

[35]Yoder 1973, 61.

[36]*QGW* II, 54-55; Wappler, 228-82; Meyer 1874, 222-44; Schmid 1971; Packull 1977, 78-87.

[37]*GZ* I, 50.

by the beginning of the persecution of Anabaptists in Switzerland in 1525. He identified this persecution with the removal of the daily sacrifice, the sacrifice of obedient suffering, the cross-bearing of the believers. He also seems to have identified the Anabaptist martyrs with the witnesses of Revelation 11. Meanwhile a man clothed in linen was baptizing (Dan. 10:5, 12:6) for one and one half years and who is identified in Daniel 12:7 as the one who announced that at the end of the three and one half years tribulation the end would come. This is almost certainly a reference to Hans Hut who began his baptizing in the fall of 1526. The abomination of desolation was the destruction of the holy place, that is, God's faithful people, but despite the persecution the church would be preserved in those three and one half years, until the number of martyrs would be fulfilled.   This brought the timetable to his own imprisonment and suffering beginning late 1527. Now the judgment on the godless would begin. They would weep for 5 months, and then, on the day of Pentecost 1528, they would see the Son of Man coming in the clouds of heaven. Then followed the resurrection, the Last Judgment, and the Seventh Day.[38] We notice that, in contrast to Hut, there is no provision in Schiemer's scheme for the vengeance of the elect.

Thus while at an important point Schiemer disagreed with Hut, he also rejected the calculations of Hubmaier which were meant to ridicule the time scheme of Hut.[39] Hubmaier had argued that the three and one half were not calendar years but sun years, each of which was equal to 365 years.[40] It appears to have been an arbitrary calculation on Hubmaier's part, designed to disparage Hut whom he detested. He obviously had no use for such calculations.

The most important and persistent calendarizer among Anabaptists was Melchior Hoffman. He began his public preaching in the early 1520s as a follower of Luther. Something in his background seems to have predisposed him in a special way to apocalyptic speculations, for in his very first writing we find him linking references in the book of Revelation to contemporary events.[41] His preaching about the nearness of the end in Dorpat, Livonia, made enemies of the evangelical clergy and led to his banishment in the summer of 1526.

---

[38]*GZ* I, 54-6; Packull 1977, 110-12.

[39]*GZ* I, 55.

[40]Hubmaier, 474-5.

[41]*Derpten*, 262-3.

But before he left, he had written his most influential work on the endtime, his commentary on Daniel XII, which was printed in Stockholm later in 1526. It offers the basic chronology of the endtime. Klaus Deppermann argues that Hoffman borrowed basic ideas and images from Luther's writings.[42] Perhaps so, but it can also be shown that he constructed the sequence of events from the biblical materials, determined in part by ongoing contemporary events.

Basic to his calculations was a trinitarian view of world history, much like that of Joachim of Fiore. He saw the three ages of the Father, Son, and Holy Spirit corresponding to the night of the Old Testament, the dawn of the New Testament, and the daybreak of the new age of the Spirit beginning with the Reformation.[43] But he also worked with the scheme of the world week. The Old Testament comprised five ages and the New Testament two, the last of which was the great Sabbath which, as in Joachim but unlike Augustine, lay within history. To each of the seven ages corresponded a specific persecution of God's people, the final one being that of the church of Rome from which came the Antichrist.[44]

As did Luther, so Hoffman found in the book of Revelation the story of the church's history from beginning to end. The first period was that of the millennium beginning with St. Paul's binding of Satan. But with the emergence of the papacy Satan was let loose.[45] The papacy introduced destructive errors such as the union of the church and the empire, the Mass, the baptism of infants, and the intercession of the saints. This transformed the church of Rome into the Antichrist.[46] But then the gospel began to be preached again and the Antichrist was severely wounded, first by John Hus[47] and then in the Reformation. The last seven years began for Hoffman in 1526. In the first three and one half the special, Spirit-filled emissaries of God would preach with great success. At the end of this period a council would take place at which the two witnesses Elijah and Enoch would testify and then be crucified.[48] Then followed the tribulation in the second three and one half years when the hellish trinity of pope (the beast), emperor (the dragon), and the

---

[42]Deppermann 1979, 67-8.

[43]*Romeren* V2b, C2a, H2a-b; *Offenbarung*, Z5b.

[44]*Offenbarung* T3a-b; *Daniel* F2b.

[45]*Offenbarung*, X4b-X5a.

[46]*Offenbarung*, P7a-P8b.

[47]Ibid., K4b.

[48]Ibid., O1b-O2a.

monks (the false prophet) would attack and seek to destroy the spiritual temple erected by the true gospel preachers. The temple would be defended by an army led by two kings, one of which would be Frederick I of Denmark. This spiritual temple Hoffman came to identify with the city of Strassburg.[49] The defence of the city would succeed. The Anabaptists themselves would not bear arms but would assist with sentry duty and work on the defences.[50]   An earthly divine kingdom would then be established.[51] The apostolic emissaries, the 144,000, would go out into the whole world and preach the gospel of perfection.[52]   Babylon, the false church, would be destroyed, and the government would be obligated to kill all false prophets.[53] Then Christ would return and the wrath against all ungodly tyrants who had hindered God's plan would be unleashed by God himself, after which Christ's eternal kingdom of peace would commence.[54]   In 1533 Hoffman announced that all this was now about to transpire for 1533 was the last of the last seven years.[55]   Even when it did not happen he continued to cling to hope, re-interpreting his complicated scheme.[56]

If Hoffman's predictions were not fulfilled in Strassburg, they had a kind of fulfillment in the Westphalian city of Münster. The Reformation had been accepted there in 1532, but Münster did not settle down simply to being a Protestant city as happened in Augsburg or Geneva. The unheard-of happened. The city moved from Catholic to Lutheran to Zwinglian to Anabaptist. The last move came in February, 1534. Melchior Hoffman's followers were to be found mostly in the Netherlands, and when his predictions were not fulfilled by the end of 1533, they turned their attention to Münster as the city God had chosen to be the New Jerusalem. Nevertheless, the Münster Anabaptists had been shaped in their expectations of the End by Hoffman. Further elaboration and modification of the endtime schema was done by Bernhard Rothmann, leading reformer, preacher, and theologian in Münster. There was a mood of expectancy beginning early 1534. It was a time of visions, miracles, and

---

[49]*QGT* VIII, 185, 393.

[50]Ibid., 444-5.

[51]*Unterrichtung*, A2a-b.

[52]*Romeren*, Z1a.

[53]*QGT* VIII, 393.

[54]*Unterrichtung*, A7b.

[55]*Unterrichtung*, A2a-b.

[56]*QGT* VIII, 255, 312. For this section see Deppermann 1979, 217-31 and Packull 1986.

portents, all interpreted by the Spirit-filled prophets led by Jan Matthijs. Rothmann wrote that what had been written about the last times in the past by people like Irenaeus and Lactantius was of virtually no use for the present.[57] So he put forward his own explanation in his writings.

History, he explained, is divided into three periods, the first from Adam to Noah, the second from Noah to the times of restitution, the third to begin very soon, the time of the new heaven and the new earth.[58] The second age was the time of the four kingdoms, the Assyrian/Babylonian, the Median/Persian, the Greek, and the Roman.[59] The last monarchy, still in place, is an unnatural mixture of spiritual and secular power, imperial-papal Christendom. The small horn of Daniel 7:8 is the pope. His triple crown is the evidence that he has usurped three kingdoms. This last earthly power is now cracking. The papal Antichrist is exposed and thrown off his throne.[60] At the same time the great restitution began with Martin Luther's preaching of the gospel.[61] With the restitution, carried forward by the Anabaptists, has come also the vengeance of God on all ungodliness.[62]

Rothmann felt compelled to provide a careful scriptural basis for the Münsterite conviction that they were in the midst of the endtime events. In his work *Concerning Divine Vengeance*[63] published in December, 1534, he urgently explained that the time of vengeance had come. He began his calculations with the three and one half years of punishment Elijah imposed on Israel (James 5:17). He noticed that in the Babylonian Exile this number three and one half was multiplied 20 times because of its greater punishment to make the 70 years of the Exile. Because of the still greater evil of the time of the Antichrist those 70 years were multiplied by 20 again to make up 1400 years, the time of the Babylonian Captivity of the church.[64] This captivity began about 100 years after the ascension of Christ. Add 100 years plus the 30 years of Christ's life to the 1400 and you get 1530, close enough to his own

---

[57]*SBR*, 337.

[58]*SBR*, 333.

[59]*SBR*, 401-04.

[60]*SBR*, 350-1.

[61]*SBR*, 219.

[62]*SBR*, 296.

[63]*Bericht van der Wrake.*

[64]*SBR*, 291-2.

time to be a reliable calculation.[65] The time of grace was now over, for even as Elijah killed the prophets of Baal after the three and one half years of divine punishment, so now after the three and one half years of the church's captivity, the time for wrath had come. The abomination of desolation was visible now, for it was the deliberate resistance to the gospel seen everywhere despite the fact that people knew what the gospel was. And even as Elijah, God's servant, executed God's wrath, so God's servants today would also now do. The warlike kingdom of David had already been established. Jan van Leiden had been proclaimed king in early September, 1534. He would now lead the elect in carrying out the annihilation of the godless with the sword.[66] When the purgation had taken place, the peaceful kingdom of Solomon, that is Christ, would begin on earth, the beginning of the third age. Then there would be one shepherd, one flock, and one language.[67]

The New Jerusalem and the established kingdom of David were destroyed in July 1535. Rothmann did not have the chance to revise his calculations since he probably died when Münster was taken, although his death was never confirmed.

4. Astrology

New interest in astrology came with the revival of humanist studies in the fifteenth century.[68] What appears to us to be contrary to the praise of human reason so prominent in the Renaissance, was not so viewed then, for astrology was part of the classical heritage which was held up as a model for the sixteenth century.[69] Certainly there were those who rejected it,[70] but despite that, astrology was immensely popular in the sixteenth century.

Astrology was important for apocalyptic because, alongside of the Scriptures, it was put into the service of calculating the end of history. While Martin Luther entertained the students at his table in Wittenberg with jokes about astrology, he also wrote the preface for one of the most important

[65]*SBR*, 316.

[66]*SBR* 296-7, 297.

[67]*SBR*, 278, 296.

[68]Shumaker 1972, 27-41.

[69]Warburg 1919, 12.

[70]Ibid., 16-26, 42-52.

astrological works of the century, *The Predictions of Johannes Lichtenberger* of 1527.[71] Christians who have the gospel don't need astrology, he wrote, but for the godless signs in the heavens and their interpretations represent a warning from God. Astrologers often err, but they are also often right. Hence, wrote Luther, I cannot reject everything that Lichtenberger writes. Philip Melanchthon, Luther's co-worker, regarded astrology as very important, and so did many other prominent persons in his time.[72]

While Anabaptists shared the many varieties of endtime expectations with their contemporaries, they did not share their interest in astrology. So far as I am aware, there is in Anabaptist writings not a single reference to astrology as such as a method for getting clarity about the events of the End.[73] On the contrary, Melchior Hoffman, the only Anabaptist who refers to astrology only to reject it, said that no one needs to go to it for light. Instead he offered the Scriptures which provide all that is needed for knowledge about the events of the End. The reason for the Anabaptist rejection of astrology is likely that all of them were strongly committed to the view that human beings were responsible for what happened in history, and that they could freely choose to do good or evil. Anabaptists rejected all determinisms including the predestinarian views of the Reformers, because these seemed to absolve human beings from responsibility for their actions.

After Münster there was very little calculation concerning the endtimes among Anabaptists as well as among other Christians. Servetus tried his hand at it as late as 1553 when, using the Scriptural number of 1260 years, he calculated that the return of Christ would take place in 1558.[74] But virtually everyone else had been burned by the experience of Münster. Along with other Christian writers, the surviving Anabaptist leaders continued to write that they expected the return of Christ to take place very soon. Menno Simons, Dirk Philips, Pilgram Marpeck, and Peter Rideman to name only a few, referred often to the endtime, but they left all calendarizing strictly alone. Although apocalyptic enjoyed a luxurious revival in English Puritanism a century later,[75] it was not until the nineteenth and twentieth centuries that Mennonites ventured to work at it again.

[71]Lichtenberger.

[72]Warburg 1919, 13; Hartfelder 1889, 237-41.

[73]But see Hoffman in *Tuchenisse* A2a; *Daniel XII* 3b; *Weyssagung* A2b.

[74]Friedmann 1978, 38.

[75]See Hill 1971.

III.   The Age of Visionaries

Before proceeding to the specific themes which characterized popular apocalyptic dreams, I would like to ground the subject of this book firmly in the religious, political, and social soil of its time, the first half of the 16th century, by means of the stories of the life and vision of four individuals.

The four portraits that follow are four of many that could have been chosen. Although *Thomas Müntzer* has come in for a great deal of attention in the last fifteen years, I tell his story, briefly, once more, because he was so important for the apocalyptic of the Radical Reformation. He first played all the apocalyptic themes with variations and provided much of the vocabulary of critique and abuse. *Hans Hergot* is much less well-known, but we can still feel the force and energy of his vision. He was certain that the injustice of his time was so great that only divine intervention could set it right. *Augustin Bader* combined elements of the vision of Müntzer and Hergot, but added to them his own bizarre touches that make him appear unbalanced and perhaps even pathological to the modern observer. I chose him rather than the fantastic Herman Schoenmaker[1] from t' Zand in Groningen, who appears merely ridiculous and preposterous even by comparison with Bader. *Jan Matthijs* came with a fierce vision of the future fed by his own resentments, and became the architect of the only actual attempt to establish the apocalyptic community of the endtime. It was Matthijs who inspired both Bernhard Rothmann and Jan van Leiden to become central figures in the drama of the city of Münster in 1534-1535. I chose him rather than Hans Hut with whom he had some important convictions in common, but whose story has already been adequately told. These stories illustrate graphically the themes to be discussed in the following chapters, and may serve as the historical anchors for the discussion of concepts and ideas.

This then is the story of four who had visions, all of whom belonged to the Radical Reformation, but only one of whom was an Anabaptist. The first, Thomas Müntzer, has often been called the father of Anabaptism. He was not

---

[1]*Dan* I, 114-119.

an Anabaptist, but he was one of their fathers in several senses, among them his visions of the end. The second, Hans Hergot, was never an Anabaptist, although he was a friend of some, and shared many of their views. The third, Augustin Bader, was an Anabaptist for a while but left them when they would not believe his visions. The last, Jan Matthijs, was the only consistent Anabaptist of the four. He actually got a chance to put his visions into practice for a little while. In the succeeding chapters many other Anabaptists and their views of the end will be discussed. But for now, the story of four men who actually lived in a time which to them was as exciting and confusing as our time is to us.

1. Thomas Müntzer

Even as in the whole Reformation we cannot avoid Martin Luther, so in the Radical Reformation we cannot avoid Thomas Müntzer. For a long time Mennonites quickly closed their eyes whenever he appeared in the field of vision of Anabaptist history and theology. They hoped he would go away and annoy someone else. Actually the Lutherans and the Calvinists felt the same way. No one wanted him. He was the self-confident skunk in the Reformation henhouse. He was not a Lutheran, neither was he a Zwinglian nor an Anabaptist. Since he carried none of the contemporary labels no one really knew what to do with him and so for a long time he was multilaterally dismissed as a thoroughly bad man. Mothers in the sixteenth century told their children that Thomas Müntzer would get them if they did not behave. To make matters worse for Christians, the Marxists loved him and made him into a hero.

However, we can learn that skunks are useful animals and accept them even though we carefully keep our distance. Likewise we have learned that Thomas Müntzer was a very important person in the sixteenthth century, and we don't have to love him to know that. In fact, the Lutherans, who hated him more than anyone else beginning with Martin Luther himself, can be credited with rehabilitating him.[2] That means that he came to be recognized as an important person of the Reformation period in his own right. But it's taken Mennonites a long time to recognize that he belongs to their history as well, whether they like it or not. That is why he deserves careful attention, and that is why he is the first of the four.

[2]Holl 1923.

Thomas Müntzer[3] was in turn a chaplain in a convent, a popular preacher and agitator in at least four places, and finally a self-appointed leader in the disastrous revolt of the peasants in 1525. But he was also a highly educated man; the one portrait we have of him shows him in a scholar's gown and hat. He was an accomplished theologian, a gifted writer, a spellbinding preacher, and a visionary. He was a father of the Radical Reformation.

Müntzer was one of the many intellectuals who joined Martin Luther in attacking the papal church in the heady early years of the Reformation. He first gained public attention and notoriety when, at the age of 32, he was preacher in one of the churches in the Saxon bordertown of Zwickau which lies about 100 miles northwest of Prague. Virtually from the beginning of his appointment in early 1520 he got into the hair of his superior John Egranus, who was preacher of the main church in the city.[4] Egranus was a humanist scholar with a cool, intellectual approach to Christian faith. Müntzer, by contrast, was passionate and reckless. For him Christian faith was not a matter of scholarly disputes but of living and acting.

Far more important for our story, however, was Müntzer's growing acquaintance and identification with a movement of lay people in the city. These people were weavers and other working people who had fallen on hard times. They were very conscious of their separation from the well-to-do privileged people especially in economic terms. They were also the carriers of an understanding of Christian faith that had been at home in Zwickau for a long time. Basic to this understanding was the belief that every person, no matter how humble, had direct access to God and all that he has to give without having to depend on a priest for it. Because most of them were illiterate, they had no direct access to God's word in the Bible, and they had long since concluded that what the priests told them could not be trusted. God must have another word for them, they said, and that is the voice of His Spirit in each person. Müntzer's own studies had already predisposed him to similar views, and he entered into the tense social situation with enthusiasm. He attacked the monks and the clergy with intemperate and incendiary language because, he said, they were nothing but deceivers and could think of nothing but to satisfy their lusts. Certainly, they did not speak for God. Rather than listening to them, people should listen to the voice of the Holy Spirit. Egranus was eventually also included in his attacks. In a letter to Müntzer of early 1521 Egranus wrote: "I've written to you in German for a good reason. I

---

[3]For the best recent description of Müntzer's life and thought see Goertz 1989.

[4]Rupp 1969, 163ff.

suspect that your Spirit despises scholarship and Scripture."[5] The scholarly language was Latin; German was considered by many to be too crude for theological discussion. It was a put-down and insult that must have made Müntzer, who knew Latin well enough, very angry.

He eventually caused such an uproar in Zwickau that he was expelled. But he already knew what he was going to do. He would go to Prague where there had been a revolt against the church a century earlier and where such opposition was still bubbling. No doubt he thought of himself as a great reformer for he said that no other human being had worked so hard to gain an unparalleled understanding of the holy Christian faith as he had.[6] Müntzer's preaching in Prague was as inflammatory as it had been in Zwickau. He railed against the clergy for hiding the truth of Christian faith from people, and sought to gain support for his views among the contending Prague factions.

In November, 1521, he made public what has become known as The Prague Manifesto. It was a call to the people of Prague to launch the true reformation, the Spirit-reformation, a reformation not tied to clergy or books, but which would teach the true faith which comes only from the cleansing work of the Spirit in the heart. He had come to Prague, he wrote, to the city of the holy champion Jan Hus, "to fill the sounding and commanding trumpet with the new praise hymn of the Holy Spirit."[7] Here the new church would begin, and from here spread to the whole world.[8] Although he had given up on the clergy, he had no doubts that the ordinary people would follow and carry it through.[9] Müntzer was very confident of his own role as the chosen instrument of God. He believed he had the "spirit of Elijah", the spirit of prophecy.[10]

> The time of harvest is at hand! That is why God himself has called me to gather it in. I have honed my sickle, and my soul is passionate for the truth. My lips, skin, hands, hair, soul, body, and life curse the unbelievers![11]

[5]*TMSB*, 368.

[6]*TMSB*, 491.

[7]*TMSB*, 495.

[8]*TMSB*, 504.

[9]Ibid., 500.

[10]Ibid., 504.

[11]Ibid.

Müntzer clearly regarded his undertaking of the work of reform as the beginning of the train of endtime events. He wrote at the end of the Manifesto that whoever despised his warning, would fall into the hands of the Turk after whose raging the true, personal Antichrist would reign. Very soon Christ would give the kingdom of this world to his elect for ever and ever.[12]

The Bohemians did not follow him and Müntzer left when growing opposition to his activities made staying impossible. He moved around for a while and gradually discovered that the new evangelicals, as Luther and his followers were called, did not want him any more than the Bohemians did. In time Luther and his fellow reformers came to be included in his violent denunciations of the clergy. On Easter Day, 1523, he became pastor in the town of Allstedt, where he had his one and only opportunity to work with some success as a reformer. Here he also began to write. His first two booklets[13] found their way in mid-1524 into the hands of Conrad Grebel and his friends in Zürich. They were attacks upon the false faith of the papal church as of the new evangelicals. In the second of the two booklets he also attacked infant baptism because it was disconnected from faith. In his preaching he proclaimed that the reformation would be brought about by ordinary people who flocked to hear him. These people, who were taught by the Holy Spirit and not by the "cursed parsons" would impose the new reform by force on those who opposed it. Together with a group of about 30 citizens he founded "The League of the Elect", a secret military organisation which was to be the spearhead of the new movement. Small wonder that the authorities became very uneasy. Duke John, in whose jurisdiction Allstedt lay, decided to find out for himself who Müntzer was and what his intentions were. He invited Müntzer to preach before him and a group of government officials. This Müntzer did on 13 July, 1524. For him it was an opportunity to enlist the Saxon authorities for his programme of establishing the reign of Christ on earth.

In this sermon he outlined, among other things, his view that they were all living in the last days and what was about to happen. It is an exposition of Daniel 2, the story of Nebuchadnezzar's vision of the great image which was destroyed by a stone. The book of Daniel was even in the sixteenth century regarded as one of the most important prophetic books. It provided Christian interpreters with the framework for the unfolding of human history, the scheme

---

[12]Ibid., 504-05.

[13]*Von dem gedichteten Glauben* and *Protestation oder Erbietung*

of the five kingdoms or monarchies. Four had gone: Babylon, Persia, Greece, and Rome. The fifth he identified as the contemporary obscene mixture of sacred and secular power in the coalition of the Holy Roman Empire and the Holy Catholic Church. The ending of this fifth monarch, he proclaimed, was in full swing. There was therefore no more time to postpone the reformation, and he urged the Princes not to listen to the "hypocritical parsons" which meant mainly Luther. The stone made without hands which would come and crush the fifth monarchy was already growing large because the ordinary people were understanding Christ and his Holy Spirit much better than the learned and powerful, and were following him. This is an important sign to the Princes, and if they could only understand what was happening and see where God was working, they would hardly be able to restrain their hands from the sword. "And don't", he warns, "give us any old jokes about how the power of God should do it without your application of the sword!"[14] Only after thoroughly cleansing the world of all unbelievers could the true reformation come. "The angels, who are already sharpening their sickles are the devoted servants of God, the elect, who carry out the zeal of God's wisdom."[15]

Müntzer saw himself as a new Daniel, even as he saw Luther, the other reformers, and the papal clergy as Nebuchadnezzar's wise men who could not help the Princes. He hinted that he should be given an official position as guide of the Princes, even as Daniel had been made "an officer in order that he might execute good, righteous decisions, as the Holy Spirit says."[16]

Müntzer was totally convinced that God was about to end things. He will, he wrote, prepare the transformation in the Last Days. He will free the world of its shame and pour out his Spirit of prophecy and vision on everybody. God has revealed this final, invincible coming transformation to his elect, the simple, ordinary people, and they know it has to be carried out. It is inevitable.[17] Nor did he shrink from the implications of his preaching. He detected the beginnings of God's final judgment in the Peasant uprising of 1524-5, and saw in the rebels God's elect who were gathering to carry out God's apocalyptic judgment on all unbelievers. He joined the peasants in

---

[14]Williams 1957, 66.

[15]*TMSB*, 262.

[16]Williams 1957, 69. The text of the sermon is found in *TMSB*, 241-63; the standard English translation in Williams 1957, 49-70.

[17]*TMSB*, 255.

1525, and was with them at the final annihilating battle at Frankenhausen where he was taken prisoner. He was executed soon after.

Müntzer was the most dramatic sixteenth century exponent and practitioner of the late medieval understanding of history. He foresaw a new order which would take over in a cleansed world after the judgments of Turk and Antichrist, and the assumption of undisputed kingship by Christ. There would be complete equality and government by ordinary people. There would be equal distribution of goods. Any opposition to the new order by the present rulers would first bring in a warning. and, if it was not heeded, death.[18]

Others would provide much more detail for the shape of the new earth, the millennium, but Müntzer influenced virtually the whole radical reformation in one way or another by his views. The Hutterite Chronicle, many years after Müntzer's death, included the following entry:

Thomas Müntzer of Allstedt, in Thuringia, was a highly intelligent and eloquent man who proclaimed many a profitable doctrine based on the Sacred Scriptures against the Catholic and the Lutheran Church. He taught of God and his quickening Word and his heavenly voice against all scribes. The people quickly accepted his teaching and opposed the Catholic priests. At that point the peasants rebelled in the land and he could not keep them in Christian peace. He was blamed by those who willed him ill for this rebellion and indicted as its originator, and was captured and beheaded by the Duke of Saxony. His head was placed on a pole. God, however, has declared and confirmed his innocence in many a pious heart.[19]

2. Hans Hergot

Almost two years after Müntzer's death another man was executed in Saxony. He was a printer and book peddler and was not involved in any revolt as Müntzer had been. One of Müntzer's works[20] against Martin Luther had been printed in Hergot's printshop in Nuremberg, but somehow he managed to

---

[18]*TMSB*, 548.

[19]Quoted in Hillerbrand 1967, 27.

[20]*Ausgedrückte Entblössung.*

avoid prosecution, perhaps because he had no reputation as a publisher of radical literature. He was put to death because it was alleged that he was the author of a little book with the title *The New Transformation of Christian Living*.[21] He had evidently had the work printed in Leipzig and had arranged for its distribution.[22] It was the content of the book that condemned Hergot. The authorities regarded it as a programme for a renewed uprising of the "common man" and overthrow of the established authorities in church and state.

The book was not apocalyptic, that is, it did not employ the usual images from Daniel and the Revelation. It provided no calendar of endtime events nor a timetable. Nevertheless, the author was convinced that he was witnessing the passing of the old sinful, corrupt order of the world and the imminent establishment of a new one. He calls his vision the "new" transformation. It was the third of three, and had not yet taken place. So it was new with reference to the two preceding transformations. But perhaps this was also meant in part to stand in contrast to the transformation that had been expected from the Reformation and especially from the peasant uprising of 1525. Thomas Müntzer had expected it then, but it had not happened because, as Müntzer said at the end, the peasants had sought their own private advantage and not the welfare of Christendom.[23]

The book has two parts. The first is a description in some detail of the new order of the world which is about to come, and the second a bitter, virulent tirade against the Protestant spiritual and secular authorities. It issued from an intense agonizing disappointment at the failure of the Reformation.

"There have been three transformation", the book begins.

The first was the way of God the Father in the Old Testament. He second transformation was the way of God the Son with the world in the New Testament. The third transformation will be that of the Holy Spirit. It will be the transformation from the evil in which they [the world] now find themselves.

[21]Steinmetz 1977.

[22]Klaassen 1987B.

[23]*TMSB*, 473.

To the honour of God and for the common good, I, an ordinary man, make known what is about to take place. God will humble all estates, the villages, castles, nunneries and monasteries, and establish a new transformation in which no one will say: "This is mine."[24]

Primeval justice and equality will be restored after the whole existing system is swept away. "Now", he writes, "things are happening. He [the common man who has the Spirit] is learning things in a way the scribes don't like. He is speaking the truth and that is what the scribes can't tolerate." The world has been brought to ruin by the arch-deceivers he refers to as scribes, the religious leaders, the doctors of Scripture. They are directly to blame for all the strife that has taken place such as the peasant revolt, and are already inciting rulers to even greater violence. These men, who in spite of all their claims to knowing the Gospel, are in reality self-deluded blind guides of the blind. They are the ones who are setting in motion the movement toward the End. God, who is in control of all events and all people, will lead the charge against these deceivers. When that movement begins it will be a lot worse than what the peasants did. God will eliminate totally all special privilege, for "God does not much care about cities and castles. But he cares for the houses in which he lives, namely the poor people . . . . He will not tolerate that they be destroyed." Since the rulers and Scripture-twisters did not receive the peasant revolt as a divine warning, they are now up against God himself. He has raised up the Turks to punish them. And not only that, but the Emperor and the Pope are at war with each other, along with their supporters, "all of them against each other and all desiring each other's blood." The strife between the two heads, or two shepherds as the author calls them, is a sign of the End. And the religious rulers are so blind that they are pleased with it, and back up each side with Scripture. Such perversion is also a sign of the End.

God will sweep away the present order, and establish a new one with a single shepherd. He will possess and be guided by the Spirit of God. So will all of those under him who will be elected rulers in the new transformation. All property and all that's needed for human life, will be held in common, and no one will lack for anything.

The book, Hergot explicitly states, is not a call for rebellion. God does not need human rebellion to carry out his purpose. But the book is inspired by the wrath of God, and the events predicted in it will inevitably happen since God is the avenger of the poor. "Whoever is innocent need have no fear. But

---

[24]Ibid., 107. Translation by W.K.

whoever is guilty, let him fly to God and beg for mercy. It is high time, for God proposes to root out the weeds . . . . We believe the voice of the Lord; it will happen as he promised."

The author tells his readers that he had made this known in God's name because, although he was an ordinary man, he could no longer hold it in. He closes with a picture to illustrate the main point of the tract. It is the vision of the three tables.

The first table is overflowing with far too much; the second is middling with enough to satisfy all needs; the third has very little. Then those from the overflowing table came and attempted to take the bread from the third table. That is the source of the conflict. God will overturn the overflowing table and the needy one, and establish the one in the middle.[25]

3.   Augustin Bader

The third man, Augustin Bader along with his vision, is even less known than the preceding two. He never achieved any prominence and we know about him only from extensive surviving records of the lengthy interrogations he and his followers endured after their arrest.[26] Like Müntzer and Hergot, Bader was executed.[27]

He appears on the stage of history as an Anabaptist in Augsburg in 1526. He came from respected social circumstances and could read and write. So could his attractive, resourceful wife Sabina, who survived her husband in a dangerous time primarily thanks to her wits. Bader was baptized in 1526 and absorbed much from his Anabaptist teachers Hans Denck and Hans Hut. Like many another Anabaptist he recanted after being arrested only to disregard his recantation promptly and continue his activity as an Anabaptist. Such behaviour was not unusual for that time, for it was acceptable ethical conduct to disregard a promise made under duress. He was ordained as a leader and baptizer and worked with some success in several centres.

[25]Translations by the author from Steinmetz 1977.

[26]Bossert 1914.

[27]For discussions of Bader: Packull 1977, 130-8; List 1973, 172-86.

The two men who influenced him most, Denck and Hut, both died late 1527. Hut had predicted that the return of Christ for judgment would take place at Pentecost, 1528. When that date passed and the expected salvation did not take place, Bader seems to have become increasingly disillusioned with his teachers and generally with Anabaptists and their teachings. Nevertheless he decided to try to win them for another vision. Meanwhile he had met the former priest, now Anabaptist, Oswald Leber. Leber had earlier participated in the Peasant Revolt. He shared with Bader his views of a coming transformation (*Veränderung*) which he had learned from some Jews who were waiting for the Messiah. This provided Bader with the stuff for a new programme. He now made specific plans to realize his new vision.

Consequently, in September, 1528, Bader arranged for a meeting of Anabaptists at Schönberg near Strassburg. Bader told the less than 20 persons present that he was a prophet who had the spirit of Elijah, and that his fervent prayer for understanding of what God intended to do was answered in visions granted him by God. He called on them to abandon baptizing and follow him in preparing for the coming transformation. All except four rejected his pleas; they did not trust his prophetic credentials.

Bader now took these four, one of whom was Leber, into his confidence. Based on calculations earlier developed by Hans Hut, he predicted that the new transformation would begin at Easter, 1530. They then seem to have decided to go out and gain support for their vision. Two went to Basel where they worked for a living and drew attention to themselves as a distinct group of dissenters. Bader himself made a journey to Teufen near Appenzell, a major centre of Anabaptism. At a meeting of about 100 persons he offered himself to them as a prophet, but they too rejected him. He responded angrily that they did not have the Spirit of God, and formally separated himself from them.

A year later in November, 1529, we find him in a village near Ulm where he had managed to get a dwelling. He called his followers together and informed them that his youngest son, six months old, was the messiah, the coming king of the transformed world. Until the child grew up, he, Bader, would be the regent. They should all go out now and announce the transformation that was to begin within four or five months. He and one of his followers now negotiated with a goldsmith the manufacture of a crown, a goblet, a sceptre, a dagger, and a ring, all in gold, and the gilding of a large sword. These were to serve as the insignia of the new order. The importance of these objective symbols was strengthened by visions seen by his follower Gall Vischer, an old man, which were confirmed by Leber. The visions may have been manufactured by Bader's clever wife, but they confirmed both Bader's claim to be a prophet and that his little son was the messiah. Very likely at Leber's urging, Bader talked to some Jewish rabbis at Leipheim nearby, who, according to later testimony, gave Bader their support.

Not long after, the man whose building Bader was renting became worried about all the coming and going and alerted the authorities. The whole group were arrested and taken to prison. Bader's wife escaped and survived. The others were interrogated, condemned, tortured, and executed, Bader with his own gilded sword.

Bader's confessions reveal the vision which he did not repudiate and for which he died. Easter 1530 would see the beginning of the three and one half years of trouble and tribulation before the new transformation would come. This tribulation would be the true baptism. During this time he would send preachers out to the four parts of the earth who would win followers, especially from among the Anabaptists. The main feature of this period would be the conquest of Europe by the Turks. This made some sense, for the seige of Vienna by the Turks had begun that September, and there was widespread doubt that Kind Ferdinand could hold it. During the time of the conquest the prophet and his growing group of followers would be preserved by God. But then the Turk would discover this group who had not submitted to him, and would make an attack upon them to exterminate them. At that point God would intervene and annihilate the Turkish army with hail, thunder, and lightening. Then all kings and rulers would be deposed by those who accepted the transformation. This part of the confession likely sealed Bader's fate, for he identified the two-headed eagle of IV Esdras (II Ezra) 11:34 with the Habsburg house with its two heads Charles V and Ferdinand I. In place of the old authorities in church and government a new leader would be elected who, together with 12 servants, would preach the transformation and teach the new truth. For a new understanding of Scripture would be revealed spiritually through Christ. All external sacraments and institutions would disappear and everyone would be taught spiritually by Christ. The acceptance of the transformation would be the true participation in the body and blood of Christ.

This would be the millennium, the 1000 years of peace and unity during which they would reign with God. Bader evidently saw himself or his son as the great elected leader. The leader would be both spiritual and secular, teaching as well as dispensing justice. But even secular justice would be spiritual with no place for the sword. There would be no sin or unrighteousness. Everything would be held in common. Bader expected that Turks, pagans, and Jews would be among those accepting the transformation.

After this sin would reign again until the day of the Lord would come. Bader did not know when that would be.[28]

4. Jan Matthijs

The last of the four is also the most problematic. Jan Matthijs had full Anabaptist credentials and that is no doubt why Mennonites have found him even more repulsive than Thomas Müntzer. Moreover, our twentieth century sensibilities, shaped as they are by scepticism and rationalism, find it almost impossible to regard him as a person of integrity and capable of reasonable reflection.

We get a first, fleeting glimpse of Jan Matthijs, a baker from the Dutch city of Haarlem, enduring the public humiliation of standing in a pillory and suffering the agony of a pierced tongue and a back bloody from flogging. The year was 1528, and the offence was some act of disrespect for the Mass. We next meet the powerful, tall man with a big black beard, who may have been in his forties, on the way from Haarlem to Amsterdam. It is October, 1533. He had given up his living as a baker, and was accompanied by a beautiful young girl. Not only had he abandoned the baker's trough; he had also jilted his aging wife. Who knows what happened in his soul between his public humiliation and his secret departure from Haarlem? It seems certain that he had been baptized by one of Melchior Hoffman's followers. We may conjecture that his earlier suffering for his faith had strengthened his determination to do something active about all that he considered wrong with the world. Perhaps it had produced the hardness and intolerance in him that tended to break out into violence when he encountered resistance. He was also frustrated and angry with what had happened to Hoffman's movement. In 1531 Hoffman had decreed that they should cease from baptism for two years because of the persecution. It had accomplished nothing. Besides, Hoffman's predictions that the end would come in 1533 had not been fulfilled. Hoffman himself was in prison and had not been set free as he had predicted. Something had to be done and Matthijs felt called by God to do it.

[28]This description is based primarily on the five confessions of Bader in Bossert, 11 (1914), 24-6, 44-9, 106-09, 119-20, 127-33.

His wife had likely rejected his claims to be a prophet called by God. Meanwhile he had met the pretty brewer's daughter. She was not only beautiful but also clever and articulate. "She knew the gospel well" says one of our sources, which seems to mean that she had a personal stake in Anabaptism and knew how to talk about it. They came to an agreement that she would be his wife and that they would leave secretly - to get away from her parents - and begin their mission in Amsterdam.

The preaching of Melchior Hoffman and his apostles had resulted in Anabaptist groups in Amsterdam and many other centres. All were expecting the End to come that year, 1533, and all believed in the special role of prophets and visionaries to whom God revealed what was to happen. There was also a lot of uncertainty. Matthijs made it his task to dispel the uncertainty and get the movement going again. His vision was clear in his mind. The world was sunk in corruption and would have to be cleansed before Christ could return to reign. The people to do the task were his elect, the baptized ones, the Anabaptists. He had personally separated himself from compromise and unbelief when he left his wife who did not believe in his mission. Now he expected everyone else to do likewise.

In Amsterdam he wasted no time. He claimed to be a prophet driven by the Holy Spirit, and that God had revealed unspeakable things to him. He also claimed to be Enoch, one of the two witnesses of Revelation 11. The other one, Elijah, was Melchior Hoffman. He was called, he told them, to reinstitute baptism immediately to prepare for God a pure people to carry out his bidding. The stormy entrance of this powerful man threw the Amsterdam group into confused panic. Hoffman had suspended baptism and they had received no other instructions. And someone else had already been designated as Enoch. It was prophet against prophet, inspiration against inspiration. Who was right? Matthijs responded to their hesitation with a violent attack. He would deliver them all to hell and the devil if they did not listen to him or recognize him as Enoch. In their agitation the Anabaptists gathered for prayer. Then a lad of 12 years came into the meeting, wished them peace and shook their hands. Their fear left them and they accepted Matthijs and became obedient to him. How do you decide between prophetic and inspirational claims if you accept their legitimacy? Can you ignore a prophet who threatens your salvation? In that situation, don't you at least hedge your bets?[29]

[29]Story reconstruction based on Obbe Philip's confession, Fast 1962, 319-40 and Kuhler 1961, 71-7.

From Amsterdam the pair headed for Leiden. There they lodged in the house of a tailor, where they met a colourful man named Jan Bockelszoon, known to history as Jan van Leiden. This man was anxious for the truth and had made a special trip to Münster, against his wife's wishes, because, he said, the gospel was preached better there than anywhere else. To him, too, Matthijs had to explain why his message was different from Hoffman's, but said that one should follow the truth above all. Jan van Leiden was convinced, and Matthijs baptized him.[30]

Immediately Matthijs began to send out apostles two by two, into the whole of the Netherlands and beyond. Jan van Leiden was sent with another to Rotterdam.[31] Others were sent to all the main centres.[32] Two Matthijs apostles had arrived in Münster on 5 January, 1534, and had succeeded almost immediately in baptizing the clergy of the city, chief among them Bernhard Rothmann.[33] By 13 January at least 1400 people had been baptized, about 25% of the population.[34]

When van Leiden returned from Rotterdam, he and his companion were immediately ordered by Matthijs to travel to Münster and deliver some important messages to the leaders there. They arrived on 13 January. The chief message they brought from Matthijs was that they were no longer to preach from the pulpits, but to abandon the churches totally.[35] It was the first step in the purification Matthijs had in mind. Through his apostles he changed both the mood and the course of events in Münster. Immediately we hear repeatedly of visions and portents, or people running through the streets crying woe! and repent! and making apocalyptic predictions, usually threats of God's impending wrath.[36]

At the beginning of February Jan van Leiden wrote a letter to Jan Matthijs requesting that he come to Münster. He responded immediately. When they came to Deventer they heard there was a riot in Münster (9-10 Feb.). Matthijs decided to stay, evidently to await news of the outcome and to that end sent

---

[30]Cornelius 1853, 370, 398.

[31]Cornelius 1853, 370.

[32]Mellink 1954, 156, 164, 170, 177, 228, 242, 256, 269, 283.

[33]Stupperich 1970, 279f.

[34]van Dülmen 1977, 289.

[35]Cornelius 1853, 371.

[36]Cornelius 1853, 13, 15; Rothmann 1970, 279f.

the letter carrier to Münster. He quickly returned with the good news that all was well and Matthijs arrived there with his wife immediately after the beginning of the seige of the city about the middle of February.[37]

Now Matthijs became the dominant figure in the city. He thought of himself as a divinely appointed deliverer. He took over the already existing conviction that Münster was appointed by God as the city of peace and safety for God's people, the New Jerusalem, but that the world would be horribly punished by Easter.[38] God, he proclaimed, desired to raise up his elect people and whoever did not have the sign of TAU would perish in the wrathful punishment of God.[39] The city would have to be purified in order to be acceptable to God. All who opposed God would have to be expelled.[40] For people from various social strata and levels of education to accept Matthijs so quickly and enthusiastically testifies to the man's strength and charisma. He was the divine oracle they craved for.[41]

Matthijs' first action was to initiate the destruction of images in the churches, indeed of everything that was reminiscent in any way of the past. The images, frescoes, stained glass windows, relics, altars, organs, furniture were smashed. Archives with their city records, bills, and contracts were looted and the contents burned. All the seals were destroyed, all letters burned.[42] Following that, on 15 March, he ordered all books except the Bibles to be brought to the cathedral square and burned. This was done, as one contemporary source reports, in order to erase all alternative interpretations of Scripture and all other knowledge so that Matthijs himself could be in complete control.[43] It was the action of a true believer. In order to establish a new order the old would have to be obliterated, "so that nothing of these things would remain in the memory of the next generation."[44] It was all done not for the fury of destroying what was not understood but for the elimination and cleansing of realities whose power was understood very well indeed.

---

[37]Cornelius 1853, 410.

[38]van Dülmen 1974, 82.

[39]Cornelius 1853, 405.

[40]van Dülmen 1974, 299.

[41]Cornelius 1853, 40.

[42]van Dülmen 1974, 90-1.

[43]van Dülmen 1974, 100.

[44]Ibid., 1974, 91.

On 23 February the Anabaptists gained control of the city through civic elections. They were now in position to take further steps in the actualization of the vision of the pure city of the elect. Two days later in a sermon Jan Matthijs said that the New Jerusalem could not maintain its new order with so much dissent, and so many opinions and sects remaining in the city. Hence, he said, it was the will of the Father that all uncleanness be removed from God's city. All Catholics, Lutherans, and others opposed to the new order should be killed. Only thus could contamination and infection be avoided. This would very likely have happened had not other leaders including Jan van Leiden intervened and warned that not only would it be barbaric to do such a thing, but it would unnecessarily provoke Münster's enemies. Instead, all unbelievers should be expelled and Münster's purity be preserved. Matthijs yielded.[45] On 27 February, when preparations for the expulsion were already under way, Matthijs ran through the streets calling on all to repent and convert. Returning to the market where armed men were assembled, he fell down breathless. Then, as though he had received a message, he jumped to his feet and said: "This is the will of the Father, that the godless who refuse baptism will be chased out of the city. Their presence soils the people of God. Drive out the children of Esau! This city belongs to the sons of Jacob, to the true Israel."[46] Many hitherto unconvinced were now baptized, but a large number who would not submit were driven out penniless in the cold of winter. Other decisions to strengthen the New Jerusalem were also carried out about this time, among them an appeal to Anabaptists in the Netherlands to come to Münster to escape the imminence of God's judgment,[47] and the institution of the community of goods.[48] This was done in imitation of the early church in Acts in the attempt to be absolutely faithful to Scripture in restoring the church to purity.

As we have seen, Jan Matthijs would brook no opposition. The military threat from the bishop's army surrounding the city made strict internal discipline necessary. Matthijs did not hesitate to exercise it. A man named Rüscher was heard to say that the prophets and preachers would prophesy until all in the city were dead and that they were possessed by the devil. He was arrested and accused of blasphemy. He admitted to having said what he was accused of. Matthijs proceeded to immediate justice and ordered him to stand

---

[45]van Dülmen 1974, 71-2.

[46]Kühler 1961, 82.

[47]van Dülmen 1974, 78-9.

[48]Ibid., 98-9.

against the wall. The man threw himself down and pleaded for his life. The Prophet took a gun and shot him in the back as he lay on the pavement. It took him eight days to die.

Matthijs was the virtual ruler in Münster for six weeks. He had predicted that the End would come on Easter Day, which that year fell on 5 April.[49] The day before at a wedding banquet he went into a trance with much movement of the head and the hands. Everything went quiet as the guests sat and watched. When he awoke he said with a sigh "O dear Father, not as I but as you will!" He got up, wished them all God's peace, and left with his wife.

Next day he went out of the city with a handful of men to attack and scatter the besieging army. His credibility as a prophet was at stake. If God now came through to help his prophet, the story would unfold as he had hoped. If not, he would not have to face his deluded followers. He and his men were killed. Matthijs was pierced with a lance and his body hacked into small pieces which the soldiers threw at each other. They put his head on a stake. They did not know who he was.[50] Even so, some in the city believed that he would arise and visibly ascend into heaven, according to Revelation 11:12.[51]

Four men who likely never met each other, but each expecting the imminent end. With it would come justice for the oppressed, the end of persecution and exploitation and economic inequality. It would give them a place to stand and would establish the dignity of lay people for all the world to see. Their voices sound strange and chaotic and perhaps even idiotic to us, and it is easy to despise them for their ignorance and naivete and adopt a superior attitude. But they were, all of them, men of deep conviction with a passion for justice. They all died a violent death. Some might have avoided it by recanting.

The themes of the three succeeding chapters, Antichrist, restitution, and the outpouring of the Holy Spirit, are all found in the four visionaries of this chapter. They were as certain as human beings could be that God would bare his own right arm for justice very soon. Hence there was an urgency about their words and actions, and excited expectation of the onset of the extraordinary events that would finally liberate all the oppressed.

[49]van Dülmen 1974, 16.

[50]Cornelius 1853, 38-39.

[51]Fast 1962, 336.

The Last Time would be the time of the great apostasy of the leaders of the church who would follow the Great Deceiver. This conviction was expressed in an intense anticlericalism, the chief note of which was that the spiritual leaders were totally untrustworthy. All of our visionaries were, therefore, champions of the priestly role of lay people.

All four shared the passionate yearning for the final transformation which was to come soon. God would bring about the overturning of the existing order and put in its place a new order of justice and peace which would never come to an end, because it would be God's doing and not part of mutable human planning and acting. It would be part of the divine summing up of history.

Finally, all believed themselves to be under the influences and guidance of the Holy Spirit who had been newly poured out in this time of the End. They greeted this coming of God with great anticipation because it was a coming especially to lay people, most of whom had no direct access to the Scriptures because they could not read. But they could in faith receive the Spirit who came with wisdom and power. This outpouring was part of the great levelling process of the End, for illiterate and underprivileged people could have faith and could therefore also be possessed by the Spirit. Müntzer, Bader, and Matthijs all considered themselves Spirit-led leaders and actors in the events of the End. They were therefore champions also of the prophetic role of lay people. There is nothing at all to suggest that they were deliberate deceivers or charlatans.

All of them died without seeing the consummation of their expectations and without seeing their own work linked directly with God's in the expected return of Christ. They were articulators of the intense yearning of ordinary people for liberation from all the age-old oppressions of the powerful.

IV. The Age of the Antichrist

No doubt virtually every Christian in North America is familiar with the concept of the Antichrist. Certainly the TV evangelists will not let us forget it and even some of the motion pictures of recent years such as *The Omen* series have dabbled in it. My own meeting with the Antichrist came in the form of a gigantic armed warrior in a book with the title *Titan the Son of Saturn*, which I read in my early teens.

People in the sixteenth century appear to have been at least as familiar with the Antichrist as we are today. The German intellectual historian Hans Preuss wrote that in the late medieval and Reformation period the discussion concerning the Antichrist was not a preserve of the scholars but was of interest to ordinary people everywhere. In the late fourteenth century it was stated that even small children would recognize the Antichrist when he came, so well was he popularly known.[1]

1. The History and Coming of the Antichrist

In the sixteenth as in previous centuries people were convinced that they were living in the age of the Antichrist. Either he was already on the scene incognito or openly, or he was about to be revealed. The biography or personal history of the Antichrist had been put together from obvious Scripture references and from less obvious ones. The standard text was written by Adso, abbott of a French monastery in the tenth century. Adso's story[2] was embellished and expanded in a print of 1505 published in Erfurt, based, according to the anonymous writer, on many books. It is a small volume with alternating text and illustrative woodcut.[3] The Antichrist is identified as a Jew, born from the tribe of Dan out of the incest of a father with his virgin daughter

[1]Preuss 1906, 41.

[2]See McGinn 1979, 82-87. See chapter I.

[3]Several of these are printed in Emmerson 1981, between pages 118 and 119. The medieval play *Ludus de Antichristo* from ca. 1160 C.E. touches on many of these themes. See J. Wright, *The Play of Antichrist*, Toronto : The Pontifical Institute of Medieval Studies, 1967.

(Gen. 49:17, Deut. 33:22, Jer. 8:16). Present at the conception is Satan himself. The Antichrist is born in Babylon, lives in Bethsaida, and is circumcised in Jerusalem. He is taught sorcery and magic in Chorazin. In Capernaum he announces his claim to be the messiah, a claim disputed by the two witnesses Enoch and Elijah. He destroys the divine books of the law, assisted by the clergy. Clad in a scholar's gown, he performs miracles. The Jews receive his sign on forehead and right hand to show that they believe him to be God, and the message is spread through the whole world by preachers in the robes of Scripture scholars. Then follows the assembling of the hosts of the Antichrist, including the lost ten tribes called the Red Jews who are Gog and Magog. Pope, bishops, and a lot of others become Antichrist's followers after they witness his miracles. All Christians who refuse to believe on him are martyred. After the Antichrist orders Enoch and Elijah killed, thus ending all true preaching, the two witnesses are raised up. Antichrist feigns death, but rises again on the third day to confirm his claim to be worshipped as God. Flames of fire fall from heaven upon all his followers. Then he summons them all to the Mount of Olives from where he intends to ascend to heaven. At that point he is slain by St. Michael, and the demons carry him off to hell.

A very dramatic story indeed, which was expanded even more in other similar literature.[4] Prophecies of his early appearance also circulated, one by the famous Johannes Lichtenberger in 1488.[5] And when Martin Luther began to make reference to the Antichrist in 1520, both fear and expectation mounted in Europe.

But Martin Luther had no interest whatever in these popular fancies. For him and for many preceding him, Antichrist was a collective power of evil rather than a person, but for all that no less visible and destructive. This power had been at work for a long time. That is also the way most Anabaptists understood the meaning of Antichrist. For they all read in the epistles of John that the Antichrist, the great opposition to Christ's reign, was present already in the early church.

After the early years Anabaptists appear to have taken their interpretation of the Antichrist's appearance in part from Sebastian Franck. His views on the subject are particularly well set out in his letter of 1531 to Johann Campanus. He put forward the view that the Antichrist began to lay the church waste immediately after the time of the Apostles, and that from that time onwards the

---

[4]See bibliography of primary sources in Emmerson 1981, 312-326.

[5]Preuss 1933, 11; Lichtenberger 1527, E4b, R2b.

true church was concealed in heaven. What was left on earth was the assembly of Antichrist, and that would last until Christ, at his return, destroyed it. Everything that happened after the Apostles was the service of the Antichrist, including the work and writings of the Church Fathers.[6] Franck conceived of the Antichrist not as a person but as that which destroyed the work of Christ and the Apostles. He disputed the view of Anabaptists who believed that the work of Antichrist began in the time of Constantine when the spiritual and secular powers were united.[7] Franck's view was taken over by Bernhard Rothmann in Münster,[8] by Menno Simons,[9] as well as by Caspar Schwenckfeld.[10] Martin Luther's view was that the work of the Antichrist had begun at least 400 years before his time. Sometimes he pushed it back to the time immediately following Gregory I, i.e., early seventh century.[11] Michael Servetus held a similar view in that he placed the church's apostasy at the time of Constantine.[12] But all of them agreed that the Antichrist was not an individual person but a composite power of all evil.

2.   The Identity of the Antichrist

This power was also identified specifically. One such identity was Islam, another the heretics, for example the Donatists.[13] From the late thirteenth century onwards specific popes or the papacy as an institution were increasingly identified as the Antichrist.[14] Among those who did so were John Wiclif and his associate John Purvey. In his *Remonstrance* of 1395 Purvey wrote:

---

[6]Williams 1957, 148-153.

[7]Ibid., 152.

[8]*SBR*, 217-218.

[9]*O.O.*, 321; *CWMS*, 775.

[10]*CS* IX, 205; XIX, 332.

[11]Preuss 1906, 159-161; Lilje 1932, 31; Hillerdal 1954, 113.

[12]Friedmann 1978, 37-38.

[13]Emmerson 1981, 64-65.

[14]Ibid., 69-70.

Thanne if the pope chalangith to have power to harme the churche, or to lette it fro the truth and fre ordenaunce of crist to go lightli and sikirli to heuene, he is an open antecrist.[15]

Purvey specifically called Innocent III the Antichrist because of the novel doctrine of transubstantiation which was made church teaching at the Fourth Lateran Council in 1215.[16] A similar identification was made by the supporters of Jan Hus in Bohemia.[17]

Thus by the time Martin Luther began to write about the papacy as the Antichrist, he was following earlier interpreters. He acknowledged this by having Purvey's commentary on the book of Revelation published in Wittenberg in 1528.[18] By 1520 Luther was publicly referring to the institution of the papacy as the Antichrist.[19] In 1521 a booklet with the title *The Passion of Christ and Antichrist* was published by Lucas Cranach and Philip Melanchthon, which clearly illustrated why Luther and his contemporaries called the papacy the Antichrist. The booklet is a series of woodcuts with a brief text, opposing Christ and Antichrist. On the left Jesus wears the crown of thorns; on the opposite page the pope wears the triple crown. Jesus washed the feet of his disciples; the pope has the emperor kiss his feet. Jesus was voluntarily poor; the pope regards wealth as his due. Jesus rode into Jerusalem on a donkey; the pope rides like an emperor with armed men. Jesus threw the traders out of the temple; the pope brings them in. In all there are 13 pairs of contrasts, Christ's passion described by quotations from Scripture, the Antichrist pope's "passion" by quotations from canon and civil law. The contrast is complete and persuasive. The papacy is in every sense the opposite of Christ and therefore it is necessarily the Antichrist.[20]

---

[15]Purvey, 44. Author's translation: "For if the pope claims to have power to harm the church or to block its way to the truth and the free ordinance of Christ so that it cannot go to heaven securely and without obstruction, he is an open Antichrist." Further statements in Purvey, 2, 31, 76.

[16]Ibid., 79.

[17]Preuss 1906, 54-62.

[18]Purvey, xiv.

[19]Hillerdal 1954, 110. See especially Dillenberger 1961, 51, 306, 439, 464; Tappert II 1967, 79, 115, 157.

[20]Scherer 1885.

This same theme was taken up by Caspar Schwenckfeld in 1530 and 1531 when he offered definitions of the Antichrist. He was reluctant to say specifically that the papacy or the church of Rome was the Antichrist, but the identification is clearly intended. Antichrist, he wrote, is a body which in its order, its economy, and its teaching and life is contrary to Christ and his wholesome and pure teaching. At the same time it pretends to be the true church of Christ.[21]

If Schwenckfeld hesitated to identify the Antichrist with the papacy or the papal church, Anabaptists had no such scruples. The reason for this is likely that they had no hope or intention for unifying the whole church such as Schwenckfeld had. They did not regard the papal church as a Christian church but as the great opponent of everything God had in mind for the world. In his first major work Melchior Hoffman labelled the pope as the one who was sitting in the place of Christ, and cited II Thessalonians 2 to prove his point. This Antichrist had been exposed by the new preaching of the Gospel, and now retaliated by killing Christ's witnesses and calling on the secular authorities for help.[22] This papal Antichrist had his servants who manned the walls of his fortress. The weapons they used were his decretals.[23] Even as God was the head of Christ, so the devil was the head of the pope and Antichrist.[24] The marks of this papal church, wrote Bernhard Rothmann, were injustice, greed, and idolatry. In it truth was called heresy and the true followers of Christ were persecuted and killed.[25] In this church neither true faith nor true works were visible. They were concerned only, wrote Rothmann, with their idols and meritorious works, which were invented by their false god, the antichrist of Rome together with his tonsured mob.[26] They had left nothing unspoiled from which fact it could only be concluded that in the papacy was to be found the abomination of desolation.[27] This is what Paul wrote about in II Thessalonians (2:4) and it was all so obvious that one could not only see but actually touch it, said Andres Keller of Rothenburg. It's important, he continued, that one get one's information about the papacy from proper sources

---

[21]*CS* III, 845; IV, 191-192. See also Klaassen 1986.

[22]Daniel XII, B2b-B4a.

[23]*Cantica canticorum*, L3b-L4b.

[24]*Offenbarung*, E6b. See also *Prophecey,* A2a.

[25]*SBR*, 219, 320, 408, 354.

[26]*SBR*, 200.

[27]*SBR*, 215-218.

and not from the corrupt chronicles.[28]   Menno Simons, too, argued that a church that was in every particular so contrary to Christ could be none other than the company of the Antichrist. For this "man of sin" had "placed himself in the temple of God, that is, in the hearts and consciences of men, or if you prefer, in the stead of God in the before-mentioned church."[29] Pilgram Marpeck also called the papal church the Antichrist.[30]   Like Menno Simons, he identified the temple in which the Antichrist took his place and which he laid waste as "the sanctuary of truthful hearts . . . the true temple of God."[31] Many other references could be added here. Anabaptists were part of the late medieval tradition that identified the Antichrist with the pope or the papal church.

But on occasion they also included the "new evangelicals", the Protestants, in their definition of the Antichrist. A number of testimonies from the early days of the Swiss Brethren movement point to Zwingli or the Zwinglian church as God's great opponent of the endtime. This is not surprising when we consider that, apart from Michael Sattler, they did not encounter the papal church as the great persecutor. While there is an allusion to the church of Rome in Grebel's words about the "anti-Christian customs of baptism and the Lord's Supper, in disrespect for the divine Word and in respect for the word of the pope",[32] it was Zwingli and his followers whom the persecuted Anabaptists of Switzerland found in the beasts, dragons, and Antichrist of the book of Revelation. Even in the passage just cited, the "antipapal preachers" are lumped with the pope as perverters of Christian truth. Conrad Grebel appears to have been particularly haunted by the monsters of the Apocalypse. Already in September, 1524, he identified the actions of Zürich's religious leaders with the "abomination of desolation."[33]   So much had been expected of Zwingli's gospel, and now it had turned into its opposite. Grebel identified Zwingli with the great beast of Revelation 13, the executor of Satan, elsewhere referred to as the Antichrist, and Zwingli's fellow clergy with the kings who give their power to the beast.[34]   These sentiments were also expressed by Johannes Brötli in a letter to the battered little congregation at Zollikon early

[28]*QGT* V, 199; Friesen and Klaassen 1982, 66.

[29]*O.O.*, 309; *CWMS*, 757.

[30]*WPM*, 45-46.

[31]*WPM*, 352.

[32]Williams 1957, 74.

[33]*QGTS* I, 12; Harder, 238.

[34]*QGTS* I, 72; Harder, 358.

in 1525,[35] and particularly by the Anabaptists of Zollikon as they marched on Zürich in July of 1525 referring to Zwingli as the great dragon of Revelation 12 who persecuted the church.[36] Other reports of apocalyptic language come from Kessler's chronicle of events in St. Gall involving Anabaptists.[37]

Martin Luther and his supporters also found themselves called the Antichrist by Anabaptists. One who did so was Melchior Rinck who lumped Lutherans and Catholics together as the Antichrist because of their anti-Christian actions.[38] A far more serious indictment of the "evangelicals" as the Antichrist appeared in Pilgram Marpeck's tract *The Exposé of the Babylonian Whore and Antichrist*. As evidence that they did the work of the Antichrist he pointed in particular to the Lutheran rationalizing of military resistance to the Emperor as a defence of Christ and the gospel.[39] Marpeck's literary opponent, Caspar Schwenckfeld, likewise included the Lutherans as part of what makes up the Antichrist based on his interpretation of Revelation 13:11.[40] Indeed, he wrote in 1544, Andreas Osiander, the Lutheran reformer of Nuremberg, had correctly interpreted that passage from Revelation but that, like the old Pharisees, he did not recognize himself to be part of it.[41] Schwenckfeld even hinted that Anabaptism might also be part of the Antichrist.[42]

It may therefore be said that in general the Radical Reformation spokesmen understood the Antichrist to be not an individual but a composite body. In this they followed the tradition which began with Tyconius and Augustine and which was adopted by the major church teachers in the Middle Ages and by the Protestant reformers. The cases of specific identification of Zwingli and Luther as the Antichrist by some Anabaptists should be linked with the oppression and persecution they experienced at their hands and not with the popular biographical Antichrist literature of the time.

[35]*QGTS* I, 46.

[36]Blanke 1961, 60-65; Peters 1972, 134-135 for an English translation of Zwingli's report of the incident.

[37]*QGTS* II, 612, 620-621. See also Blanke 1952, 6, note 12.

[38]*TA Hesse*, 4, 31, 33.

[39]*Aufdeckung*, A3a-A3b. See Klaassen 1987 for a discussion of this tract.

[40]*CS* XIX, 339, 341.

[41]*CS* IX, 208.

[42]*CS* XIX, 356. See Klaassen 1986, 32.

The other major candidate for the role of the Antichrist were the Ottoman Turks. Those who did not regard the Antichrist as a specific person could call both pope and Turk Antichrist without contradiction. Martin Luther wrote about the Turk as the Antichrist even while he used that term for the papacy. He did say that when one compared the Turk with the papacy, it was the papacy that won the title.[43] Elsewhere he said that Scripture predicted the coming of two cruel tyrants who would lay Christendom waste before the Last Day, one a spiritual tyrant, the pope who came with a spurious gospel; the other external and material, coming with the killing sword, the Turk. It was all one Antichrist, however. The pope was the soul, the Turk the body of Antichrist.[44]

But Luther was not the first to make the identification. Since the days of Mohammed the Muslims had been called infidels, the unfaithful ones. There was a sense of religious kinship with them since they were not generally lumped with the "heathen". Since 1453 Muslim and Turk were synonymous in the European imagination. The Turks were the greatest threat to and foes of Christendom. Already when Johannes Lichtenberger first published his great astrological work in 1488 he quoted the prophecy of the Lollard Reinhard that the Turks would come and flood over the German lands. These people, he wrote, were the descendants of Hagar, wild people who made their living as bandits, and who would soon oppress the Christians as a punishment from God. Ultimately they would be defeated at Cologne according to a prophecy of Merlin.[45] The strange social and religious customs of the Turks were regarded as evidence of their unbelief. In his panegyric on the teachings of Luther of 1522, Michael Stiefel expressed his belief that the Turks were part of the apocalyptic events of his time.[46]

But it was Justus Jonas, a professor of law at the University of Wittenberg and a Lutheran reformer who, in 1530, wrote a comprehensive treatment of the role of the Turk in the Last Days based on Daniel 7. The work was dedicated to the Elector Philip of Hesse. In the introduction Jonas wrote that the Turkish kingdom was not a kingdom like all the others because it was under God's special condemnation. It had its origin in Satan as could be seen by its moral

---

[43]Preuss 1906, 171-175.

[44]Hillerdal 1954, 111. See also Buchanan 1956, 156-159, which includes a survey of the literature on Luther's view of the Turks on page 145, note 1.

[45]*Lichtenberger*, M3b-M4b.

[46]Peuckert 1966, 170.

degradation. Its norms were blasphemy, murder, daily adultery, prostitution, robbery, arson, homosexuality, and every other vice.[47]   Jonas identified the Turk with the little horn of Daniel 7:9-14. It was mightier than all others, and had taken over Egypt, Asia, and Greece. In an interesting historical judgment, Jonas blamed Arius for making it easy for Jews and Christians to follow Mohammed. Then he proceeded to identify the Turks with the peoples who, according to old legend, had been enclosed in the Caucasus Mountains by Alexander the Great.[48]   These peoples were Gog and Magog, and it was Mohammed who showed them a hole through which they could escape. He characterized Islam as works righteousness like Anabaptism, and therefore the reports of their honourable living, if they were true, were beside the point. They refused just war rules and were wanton destroyers.[49]   They would attempt to conquer Germany but they would not succeed. Because they blasphemed God he would destroy them.

The threat of the Turks was on everyone's mind, and it is therefore not surprising that Anabaptists also frequently spoke about it, especially in the early years of the movement. One of Hans Hut's converts, Ambrosius Spitelmeier, stated late in 1527 that God would awaken the Turks against Europe as part of the woes of the last three and one half years.[50] A similar statement by an unnamed Anabaptist reflected that when the Turks came, one of them would kill a thousand, and a thousand one hundred thousand.[51] Within the next half year, said Jorg von Passau in February, 1528, the Turks would come, part of the evil forces of the endtime who would afflict the godless. But they would themselves be destroyed in a time of terrible trial.[52] These ordinary Anabaptists in Franconia and Thuringia normally did not refer to the Turk as the Antichrist. Rather, the Turk's coming was a sign that the end was near.[53] Apart from these only Melchior Hoffman of the major Anabaptist writers seriously included the Turks in his endtime scheme. He also did not refer to the Turks as the Antichrist, but as the nations of Gog and Magog, the great endtime scourge of God. These were, of course, always regarded as the

---

[47]Jonas 1530, A1b-A3a.

[48]See Anderson 1932.

[49]Jonas 1530, B4b-F3b.

[50]*QGW* II, 55.

[51]Ibid., 66.

[52]*QGW* II, 112.

[53]See frequent references to the Turks among Hut's followers in Wappler 1913, 231, 235, 242, 243, 244, 280, 282.

forces of the Antichrist. They would, in the end, also be destroyed by God.[54] That was written in 1530. In his first major work, the commentary on Daniel XII, 1526, Hoffman did not identify the Turks with Gog and Magog; in fact he did not mention them.[55] The works published in 1530 were written at a time when the Turkish threat was still high[56] and after Hoffman had become acquainted with the apocalyptic of the Hut group.

3.   The Marks of the Antichrist

This Antichrist with whom the Anabaptists and others in the Radical Reformation became acquainted was not abstract. Rather there was widespread consensus as to what the marks were by which he could easily be identified. These marks were the apostasy of the scholars, the persecution of the true Christians, commitment to violence, and the perversion of the sacraments.

a. The Apostasy of the Scholars

Anticlericalism had been a feature of church life in the Middle Ages. In the year 1296 Pope Boniface VIII issued his famous bull *Clericis Laicos* which opened with the words: "The history of olden time teaches, and daily experience proves, that the laity have always felt hostile to the clergy and have constantly striven to overstep their bounds by wickedness and disobedience."[57] It is true that he was here specifically referring to King Philip IV of France, but his words can safely serve us as an accurate general statement as well. Anticlericalism, censure of and opposition to the clergy by ordinary lay people became a serious problem for the church in the twelfth century when it reached the apex of its power and wealth. Lay people charged that the clergy were no longer simple, poor, celibate, and obedient followers of Jesus but that they were corrupted by wealth and privilege.[58] Ancient views that morally compromised clergy could not effectively administer the sacraments[59] revived. Thus clergy could not be trusted to teach and preach the truth. It was an important factor in the defection of many ordinary people from the Church during the sixteenth century. The scholars and professors of the Church

---

[54]*Weyssagung*, B2b, B4b; *Prophecey*, B4a.

[55]*Daniel XII*, G3a, K3a.

[56]The Turks abandoned the seige of Vienna in October, 1529.

[57]Fremantle 1956, 71.

[58]Sanchez 1972, 23-33.

[59]Ibid., 28-29.

endured this same attack. Already in 1439 a popular tract named *The Reformation of Sigismund* called for the reform of the clerical estate, especially by depriving it of its excessive wealth and power, and calling it to be an example of Christ's poverty and obedience. But the chief opponents to such reform, wrote the author, were the clergy themselves.[60] When the peasants presented their grievances in the Twelve Articles in 1525 they began with the demand to be able to choose their own pastors so as to ensure that they would be told the truth.

The apostasy, falling away from the truth, of the clerical leaders and scholars was widely regarded as one of the marks of the reign of the Antichrist. Late medieval woodcuts illustrating books on the Antichrist invariably showed scholars as the partisans of Antichrist. When Conrad Grebel and his friends wrote to Thomas Müntzer in September, 1524, they charged that Zwingli and his fellow clergy had forsaken the truth.[61] It was a matter of great concern to Grebel, for he returned to it again and again in his letters to his brother-in-law Joachim von Watt. He was urgent and passionate about the truth of the Gospel and almost in a panic over its perversion by the clerical scholars of Zürich:

> As Daniel prophesies, there will be in the temple an abomination of desolation, and the desolation will persist until the consummation and end, for according to Ezekiel [34:18b-19a], when they drink the purest water, they muddy the rest with their feet, and the sheep feed on that which has been trampled by their feet, and they drink what their feet have muddied. They lay out plans, not by the Spirit of God. They take counsel and not from God, so that sin is added to sin, so that they descend into Egypt without consulting the mouth of the Lord.[62]

In a later letter he included Luther in his condemnation.[63]

Other Anabaptist writers also linked the apostasy of the scholars with the Antichrist and his destructions. Hoffman wrote that the Antichrist had seduced a third of the teachers of the church. These are the stars that were swept from the heaven of the church by the tail of the dragon (Rev. 12:4). These teachers

---

[60]*Sigismundi,* A2b-C2a, D3a; Strauss 1971, 8-16, 31.

[61]Williams 1957, 74, 77, 78, 82, 85; Klaassen 1987A.

[62]*QGTS* I, 12; Harder, 283.

[63]*QGTS* I, 22; Harder, 296.

are the ones who depend on secular power for their security. Through their wisdom they obscure the Word of God so that it is not accessible to people any longer. In its place they teach falsehood.[64] Plain Scripture is not forthcoming to support the doctrines of these false teachers, wrote Pilgram Marpeck. Unable to accomplish it by Scripture, they resort to human wisdom, "all of which the Antichrist does for the preservation of his abomination."[65] When the dragon, the papal church, became aware that he was being exposed Marpeck wrote elsewhere, he raised up his own prophets (Marpeck means the Reformers) to cover over and obscure the mystery of iniquity with a spurious sanctity and through skill in the Scriptures, once again to justify false teaching regarding baptism and the Lord's Supper.[66] Bernhard Rothmann wrote that the church, from the end of the apostolic era, had fallen into complete error. None of the post-apostolic writers wrote reliably. They sought fame and praise for their wisdom, and so the simple, pure teaching of Christ was completely displaced by the theologians, decretals, and councils. The Scriptures were ignored. The same was true of the popes and the universities. They all fell away and became the abominating sacrilege which took the place of Christ. This Antichrist has been exposed in the new preaching of the Gospel through the simple, uneducated people.[67] Menno Simons repeated many of these same sentiments,[68] as also did Caspar Schwenckfeld.[69] Dirk Philips specifically linked the despising and perversion of the counsel of God by the scholars to the work of the Antichrist.[70]

The people of the Radical Reformation often found themselves the victims of scholarly devices used by both Catholic and Protestant scholars in controversies over the meaning of Scripture. Such devices were used, it appeared to them, to twist and subvert the simple, plain meaning of Scripture, and to nullify the demands of Christian discipleship.[71] When the clear, plain

---

[64]*Lifland*, A3a-A3b; *Cantica canticorum*, F4b; *Prophecey*, A4b; *Judas*, D3a.

[65]*WPM*, 54.

[66]*Aufdeckung*, A3a.

[67]*SBR*, 217-219.

[68]*O.O.*, 444, 607, 618; *CWMS*, 303, 927, 943.

[69]*CS* X, 112-114.

[70]Philips 1978, 35.

[71]See for example the long dispute about baptism in *QGTS* IV, 362-398 as an example of the kind of thing Anabaptists objected to. See also *SBR*, 338, 397.

words of Scripture could be baldly denied and turned into something else, one had to conclude that the Antichrist was at work.

b. Persecution of the true Christians

A favourite medieval scheme for sketching Christian history was to divide it into a series of persecutions. Gerhoh von Reichersberg (d. 1169) believed that the Antichrist had afflicted the church with three persecutions, the first by the Roman Empire, the second by the heretics, and the third by the simoniacs and greedy within the church.[72]   His younger contemporary, the famous bishop Otto von Freising (d. 1158), saw four such persecutions. The first was the early period ending with the accession of Constantine, the second the persecution of the orthodox by the heretics, chiefly the Arian monarchs, the third that of the hypocrites who afflicted and destroyed the church from within, and the fourth that of the Antichrist at the End.[73]   Angelo of Clareno, a spiritual Franciscan, wrote about the history of the church as a series of seven persecutions, the last one being their own persecution at the hands of the Papacy.[74] Even the powerful papal church saw itself under assault by Jews, Muslims, heretics, hypocrites, and demons, as a late fifteenth century woodcut illustrates.

It therefore comes as no surprise that Anabaptists and their kin should use similar language. They, of course, had the additional reason of actually being persecuted, and this time by those who claimed to be orthodox Christians. Persecution by pagan emperors was to be expected, but persecution of the godly by the church itself was so total a reversal of what should have been that it could only be regarded as a sign of the End. They believed that the use of force in matters of faith was a mark of the Antichrist.

It was the fourth century North African theologian Tyconius who first explained how the church could become a persecutor.   Tyconius was a Donatist, a member of a large group of North African churches who disagreed strongly with Rome on church discipline issues.   After attempts at persuasion, the church finally resorted to using the military power of the Christian empire to coerce the Donatists back to orthodoxy.   He wrote that the Antichrist could fully develop only with the use of force and violence, and that was supplied by

[72]Classen 1969, 155.

[73]Rauh 1973, 349.

[74]Reeves 1969, 191-193. A similar view seems to be echoed in Hoffman, *Daniel* XII, F2b.

government. Together the persecutors were the hypocrites who led Christ to crucifixion. The governments were the instruments and allies of the false priests.[75]   This argument was never absent throughout the Middle Ages. Many Christians disputed the church's right to impose its teachings by force. Jan Hus wrote that the papal tendency to enforce its edicts with violence was a special sign of Antichrist behaviour.[76]   Using force to spread his teaching is a sign that he belongs to the devil, wrote Justus Jonas about Islam. Christians should flee from any teacher who does likewise.[77]

It was this alliance between church and secular power with its legitimation of the use of force against dissenters that led to the Anabaptist separation of the powers of church and government.[78] Participation in that alliance, judged the framers of the Schleitheim Articles, was a fatal compromise with evil because it fundamentally perverted the gospel.

It was Pilgram Marpeck who stated the matter quite clearly and directly:

Among the ancient Christians from the time of the Apostles until the Emperor Constantine, physical force and the use of the sword among Christians was unknown, nor was it allowed them by command of their Master. Only the sword of the Word was to be used. Anyone who, after sufficient teaching, would not accept that was regarded as a pagan and unbeliever. But when the pope, at that time a servant in the church, claiming to act with the mind of Christ, was married to that Leviathan, the secular power, at that moment the Antichrist was made and born as has now been revealed.[79]

For Marpeck it was not only that the church had no right to use the secular sword. The church became the Antichrist especially when it justified that use by appeal to Christ. And by this rule he called the Protestants the "new" Antichrist since they did the same thing.[80] A very similar argument was made by Marpeck's great critic Caspar Schwenckfeld. Anyone, he wrote, who,

[75]Rauh 1973, 116.

[76]Preuss 1906, 52-53.

[77]Jonas 1530, D2a.

[78]Klaassen 1987C.

[79]*Aufdeckung,* C2b-C3a, D2a.

[80]Ibid., C3a.

appearing to be godly and pious, persecutes the spirit of Christ is an Antichrist.[81]   Menno Simons too, repeatedly made the same point.   If magistrates, he wrote in 1554, understood Christ and his kingdom, they would choose death rather than intrude the worldly sword into spiritual matters which God alone judges.   But the clergy teach them that they can do it and still be Christians.[82] Those who seek to make valid their faith and conduct with the sword are sectarians who are outside of Christ and his Word. Among others he named as his prime exhibits Roman Catholics, Lutherans, Zwinglians, and Münsterites. Thus, although Menno did not specifically identify this use of the sword as the work of Antichrist, it was clearly implied.[83]

c. Commitment to Violence

As already noted, the use of force in matters of faith, especially under the guise of the gospel, was viewed as such a radical departure from Christ by most Anabaptists as to identify it as a mark of the Antichrist.   Hence their experience of persecution was viewed in the same light. They knew, of course, that there had been persecution of Christians from the beginning, and therefore had, so far, not been a mark of the End. But now it was one of a number of signs according to Matthew 24:9-12. The Anabaptists who marched into Zürich from Zollikon in July, 1525, called Zwingli the dragon of Revelation 12. In that passage the dragon is specifically the persecutor of the church. Since the true church in Zollikon was being persecuted to extinction at that very time, it was evident to those people that the End was near.[84]   Conrad Grebel writing to his brother-in-law about the same time linked the innocent suffering of his Christian brothers with the "great day of the Lord" (2 Peter 3:10) when they would be proved innocent.[85]   In the last days, those who opposed and fought against the children of God would be given the power and authority to do so, wrote an anonymous Anabaptist in 1528.[86]   Melchior Hoffman expected the final persecution of God's people to begin very soon. Its onset would be a sign of the nearness of the final salvation. This would be cause for rejoicing and for watchfulness lest they be overcome by the suffering.[87]   "The horrible

---

[81]*CS* X, 113; IV, 190; XI, 366-367.

[82]*O.O.*, 323; *CWMS*, 779.

[83]*O.O.*, 42; *CWMS*, 75.

[84]Blanke 1952, 6.

[85]*QGTS* I, 78; Harder, 378.

[86]*Sendbrieff* 1528, E1a.

[87]*Lifland,* A2b; *Offenbarung* 1530, D2a-D2b.

raging dragon has opened its jaws wide to devour the woman robed with the sun," wrote Jacob Hutter in a letter of 1535. Like Grebel, he appears to have been especially haunted by the images of the fierce destroying beasts and monsters of IV Esdras, Daniel and The Revelation, eagles, wolves, lions, and bears, who "tear the lambs of Christ to pieces."[88] In February, 1535, Rothmann's work *The Mystery of Scripture*[89] was published in Münster. Although the mood in the city was still belligerent and truculent, Rothmann became very sombre towards the end of his hurriedly written tract. He saw the people of Münster belonging to the centuries-long succession of the bleeding witnesses of Christ, victims of the persecution of the Antichrist. Several times he expressed their willingness to suffer whatever God would lay on them.[90]

Several years later Ulrich Stadler wrote that the Hutterite community in Moravia was the place of safety given to the church to await the Lord through the final tribulation until she would be received into eternal joy.[91]   Both Menno Simons and Caspar Schwenckfeld regarded the persecution of their day as the mark of the Antichrist. This final persecution would continue until the Lord would slay the Antichrist with the breath of his mouth (II Thessalonians 2:8).[92] There were many martyrs in this "final" persecution. But martyrdom was not an end; it was a beginning. It was seen by Anabaptists as participation in the events of the End, and the fiercer the persecution, the nearer they were to the return of Christ and their glorious salvation.

d. The Perversion of the Sacraments

The third, and perhaps the most important sign of the reign of the Antichrist was the destruction or at least the perversion of the true baptism and Lord's Supper. This conviction, too, the Radical Reformation shared, at least in part, with the Reformers. Luther and Zwingli rejected the teaching of the sacrifice of the Mass since it contradicted the plain teaching of Scripture that the only sacrifice for sin had been made once and for all by Christ. About baptism Luther believed that it had been preserved intact throughout the centuries. Zwingli had some initial doubts about it but then also continued the ancient practice. Of the Radical Reformation, especially Anabaptists came with

---

[88]Hutter 1979, 154, 87, 7, 8; *Hut. Ep.* I, 152.

[89]*Van Verborgenheit der Schrifft.*

[90]*SBR*, 337, 368.

[91]Williams 1957, 281-282.

[92]*O.O.*, 301; *CWMS*, 744; *CS* XV, 194.

a much more drastic critique. In this they were perhaps more the inheritors of the medieval anticlerical tradition than of the Reformation.[93]

The identification of the perversion of true baptism and Lord's Supper with the work of Antichrist is found throughout early Anabaptism. Commenting on the Muslim assault on Vienna in 1529, Wolfgang Brandhuber wrote that in this event would be revealed the name of the beast since its marks are already in part known to us. They are the two dead elements, the senseless confirming of the child on the forehead, and the dead element, the bread in the Mass." The restoration of true baptism and Lord's Supper was seen as part of the restitution of the true and pure church in preparation for the return of Christ.

i.   Lord's Supper

Of the sacraments it was the Lord's Supper that received first attention in the Reformation. Martin Luther dealt with it in his work *The Babylonian Captivity of the Church*. In Zürich it was first discussed publicly early 1523.[94] When, later in October of that year no action had been taken after the Mass had been declared unscriptural, some of Zwingli's younger followers grew very frustrated. This led one of them, Conrad Grebel, to write in September, 1524, about the Mass as Antichrist's usage.[95] Grebel picked this language up from Zwingli's own words at the October Disputation when Zwingli referred to the Mass as "a work of Antichrist."[96] Even more extensive and certainly more extreme is the language used by the author of *The Satisfaction of Christ*. The beast, the Roman church, recuperated from the mortal wound (Rev. 13:3) which the Reformation had inflicted upon it, when the scribes, that is, the Reformers, resumed the defense of the "Bread-Lord-God", that is, the bread in the Mass. Now they too fulfilled Jesus' prediction by saying "Here is Christ" either by pointing to the sacred wafer or to a harmless, undemanding Christ.[97] When therefore the writer warned his readers to leave Babylon, it was not merely to avoid teachings with which they disagreed, but not to have anything to do with this last and final assault upon God and his little church. The anonymous Anabaptist confession from perhaps a few years later made the same point:

[93]See Moore 1975, 17, 46-60; Lambert 1977, 50, 53, 62, 80, 225-226, 269.

[94]Peters 1972, 112. This was the 18th of Zwingli's 67 Articles.

[95]*QGTS* I, 14, 18; Harder, 286, 291.

[96]Ziegler 1969, 38.

[97]Yoder 1973, 117-118.

We contradict and reject the dreadful blasphemy and more than pagan idolatry of the depraved Antichrist who seduces people to believe that Christ is bodily in the bread of their altar when the five words are mumbled over it.[98] (The five words were *"hoc est enim corpus meum"*.)

Melchior Hoffman identified the sacrifice of Christ in the Mass with the "continual burnt offering" of Daniel 12:11, and which he saw as the abomination of desolation, the Antichrist in the holy place.[99] The Mass as the specific place where the Antichrist had taken his seat was described especially by Peter Riedemann in his first *Account*. He compared Jesus' words and actions at the Last Supper with the words and actions of the Mass and set up five opposites in word and action to show the absolute contrast between Christ and Antichrist.[100] Menno Simons brought it all together in a concise statement in his *Foundation of Christian Doctrine*:

Since the adversary [Antichrist] of Christ has been on the [papal] (this word is omitted in the Verduin translation) throne for so long a time he has altered the laws of the Most High as set forth in Scripture and has instituted his abomination of desolation in their stead. He has corrupted the Holy Supper with his councils, violence, and false doctrine, till alas, it has retained only the shadow and the mere name. This they have instituted unto the destruction and corruption of the true eternal sacrifice of Christ which alone is effective before God, changing it into a daily sacrifice for sin, as may plainly be read in the canons of the mass. This undoubtedly is an abomination of abominations . . . . In this way Antichrist has bewitched the whole world with his sacrifice.[101]

In another place he says very similar things complete with references to the "Apocalyptic Apollyon" and the whore of Babylon about the Protestant Lord's Supper, echoing the author of *The Satisfaction of Christ*.[102] For Caspar Schwenckfeld the perversion of the Lord's Supper was the work of

---

[98]Hillerbrand 1959, 44-45.

[99]*Prophecey*, C3b; *Offenbarung*, B3b.

[100]*GZ* II, 34-35.

[101]*O.O.*, 29-30; *CWMS*, 151-152.

[102]*O.O.*, 469-470; *CWMS*, 516-517.

Antichrist in a special way. It consisted of worshipping a material creature, the bread of the eucharist, as God, who is only and always spirit.[103]

ii. Baptism

Although questions were raised in the Reformation by a number of people about the traditional practice of baptism[104] it was only the Anabaptists who pointed to the traditional baptism as a mark of the Antichrist. As in so many other matters, it may well be that it was Thomas Müntzer who first expressed this conviction. In his *Protestation*, which significantly influenced the Grebel circle in 1524, he wrote that the perversion of baptism was the "primeval soup" out of which all other errors came. It had happened when they made "innocent children into Christians, and Christians became children." It was, he wrote, the work of the Babylonian whore, and in the margin he cited Matthew 24, the abomination of desolation, always a synonym for the Antichrist.[105] These views were repeated or alluded to in the letter Grebel and his friends wrote to Müntzer in September, 1524, and elsewhere in Grebel's correspondence.[106] Felix Mantz said that infant baptism was invented by the Antichrist, the pope and his followers.[107] In the public argument that developed when Georg Blaurock took over the pulpit in Hinwil, he charged the Zwinglian pastor, who said he would defend infant baptism, with being the Antichrist.[108] The essence of the perversion of baptism according to the Zürich Anabaptists was that faith had been separated from baptism, and that baptism in infancy preempted any personal decision to be a Christian, and voluntarily and intelligently assume the liberation and obligation of being a Christian.[109] Balthasar Hubmaier, who was not given to using apocalyptic language, repeatedly referred to the Roman church as the Antichrist because of its perversion of baptism. He saw the work of Antichrist especially in the

---

[103]*CS* II, 453-454; IX, 205, 900; XIX, 322, 343, 356; XII, 766. See especially Klaassen 1986, where Schwenckfeld's position is described in detail.

[104]Zwickau Prophets: Wappler 1966, 84; Karlstadt: Pater 1984, 99-114; Zwingli: Goeters 1957, 47; Peters 1972, 117; *QGTS* I, 53; *ZSW* IV, 228 note 21.

[105]*TMSB*, 526, 228-230.

[106]*QGTS* I, 13, 18, 23; Harder, 286, 288, 291.

[107]Ibid., 23.

[108]Ibid., 388.

[109]Klaassen 1987a.

subversion of mutual discipline in the church, an obligation that was a direct consequence of adult believers' baptism.[110]

The Anabaptist writer who most clearly and persuasively wrote on this point was Pilgram Marpeck. Like others before him, he referred to the practice of infant baptism as the "mystery of wickedness" (II Thess. 2:7). For him the destruction of baptism consisted primarily of making sinners of innocent children,[111] and in thinking that it is possible to make Christians by baptizing infants. This, he wrote, is very nearly the root of all other idolatry and apostasy.[112] In his 1542 reworking of Bernhard Rothmann's *Confession of Two Sacraments*,[113] Marpeck added several sentences which could be regarded as a summary of his position:

> Infant baptism is an introduction into the realm of the Antichrist, a true and real entrance, beginning, door, and reason for its being, and an instigation to all evil and idolatry which is maintained through his deceptive guise of Christ, a secure anchor to deceive the people. As soon as infant baptism were to be abolished, the disruption of the realm of the Antichrist would immediately follow. The devil has undermined the true Christian baptism and done away with it. Consequently, the Christian church has become desolated and soiled and, because of infant baptism, has, instead, planted the kingdom of the Antichrist. The abolition of infant baptism, based on faith in Christ, would destroy the kingdom of the Antichrist.[114]

These statements and many others like them[115] bear eloquent testimony to the fact that the passionate condemnation of the baptism of infants was much more than cramped biblicism. It was part of a far-ranging and sophisticated reading of church history as well as a responsible attempt to read the signs of their times.

---

[110]Hubmaier, 345.

[111]*QGT* VII, 495-498; *WPM*, 145. Cf. *WPM*, 45-46.

[112]*QGT* VII, 458; *WPM*, 130, 207.

[113]See Wray 1956.

[114]*WPM*, 259-260.

[115]Hoffman: *QGT* VII, 184; Rothmann: *SBR*, 135, 160; Menno Simons: *O.O.*, 16, 301, 321; *CWMS*, 128, 743, 775.

The Anabaptists, even those most preoccupied with the detailed apocalyptic scenario, had no interest in the older, popular personal Antichrist, even though the literature promoting it was in plentiful circulation. This too is evidence of a careful reading of church history. Their Antichrist was a composite and personification of all the cumulative distortion and perversion of the true Christian faith from the time of the Apostles to their time. In their own time, they believed, it had assumed its most virulent form in the apostasy of the scholars who had been called to speak the truth, in the church's persecution of the true disciples of Christ, in the use of violence to put down dissent, and in the perversion of the central symbols of baptism and the Lord's Supper. The Antichrist was the symbol and embodiment of an escalation of perversion, corruption, and evil that had suddenly been revealed to many in the early sixteenth century.

The model for their Antichrist was the figure of the hellenistic king Antiochus IV Epiphanes who, in the year 167 B.C.E. sought to make Greeks out of the Jews by subverting their faith and desecrating their temple in Jerusalem with an image of Zeus. This was the figure Paul had in mind in II Thess. 2. The original passage in Daniel 9:27 was available to Christians, and, following Jerome in his Daniel commentary[116] they took this figure also to be a future one.

The use of the figure of the Antichrist for what Anabaptists saw as the perversion and destruction of the faith of the early church, shows just how serious they were about the issues of their time. Their use of apocalyptic language was, as I have sought to show, part of the vocabulary generally in use to deal with events of unusual magnitude and far-reaching consequences.

---

[116]See Archer 1958.

V. The Age of Restitution

The third chapter of the Acts of the Apostles contains some sentences that could serve as the basic schema for endtime expectations in the Radical Reformation. They are part of an address given by Peter following a miraculous cure in the temple and the subsequent excitement. It happened, said Peter, because of what God had begun to do "in the last days" (Acts 2:17), starting with the execution and resurrection of Jesus. These are the words according to the Jerusalem Bible:

Now I know, brothers, that neither you nor your leaders had any idea what you were really doing; this was the way God carried out what he had foretold, when he said through all the prophets that his Messiah would suffer. Now you must repent and turn to God, so that the Lord may send the time of comfort. Then he will send you the Messiah he has predestined, that is Jesus, whom heaven must keep till the universal restoration comes which God proclaimed, speaking through his holy prophets. Moses, for example, said: The Lord God will raise up a prophet like myself for you, from among your own brothers, you must listen to whatever he tells you. The man who does not listen to that prophet is to be cut off from the people. In fact, all the prophets that have ever spoken, from Samuel onward, have predicted these days. (Acts 3:17-24).

The fact that Anabaptists did not quote this passage much does not minimize its importance for our story. They held to the convictions expressed in it with persistent and stubborn passion. Let me now rephrase that passage as I imagine the adherents of the Radical Reformation might have heard it, convinced as they were that they were living at the end of the ages:

The past is past. We again hear the Gospel of God's salvation through the suffering of Christ. Now all should repent of their sins, so that they may be totally removed. The actual literal purification from sin is the condition for the times of comfort, of refreshing, of revival. When that condition has come God will send Christ to us again. He will restore all things, the whole world, to their original perfection and innocence. But all this will happen only if we listen to Jesus and do what he said. Those who will not listen are excluded from the restoration. The whole of the Scriptures testify to this universal restoration.

They were convinced that they were living in the dawn of eternity which would succeed time, the point at which all the fragments of God's creation, all that was broken and wasted and scattered and soiled and defaced by sin, was beginning to be reassembled in the new creation.

1. The Restitution of the Church

The word restitution in the title comes from the Latin translation of Acts 3:21, *in tempora restitutionis omnium*, "in times of the restitution of all things." The word restitution was used by relatively few writers in the Radical Reformation; the conviction about its content and meaning was shared in varying ways and degrees by virtually all.[1] Restoration, the reader may recall, was the expectation and hope of all four of the visionaries whose stories are related in chapter III.

But if there was to be a restitution there had first of all to be a fall from a primeval state of perfection. The writings of the Radical Reformation contain numerous litanies detailing the corruption of the world and the church. It was all part of a vast indictment of the church begun with Tyconius in the fourth century for its evil and apostasy. It increased in volume and intensity from the twelfth century onwards. Many prophecies circulating in the fifteenth and sixteenth centuries predicted a downfall of the church or at least a terrible punishment for its sins. The chief target were the clergy whose sins of greed, lust, abuse of power, and despising of holy things were itemized over and over again.[2] One of the strongest condemnations of the corruption of the church comes from the fifteenth century and has been attributed, perhaps wrongly, to Johann von Wesel. The church, that author wrote, has become legalistic. It is nothing but empty, faithless boasting about works. The clergy are concerned only about money and their own private interests and neglect their true vocation. And the ordinary people are deprived and perish from lack of spiritual food. Either these agents of unrighteousness, these gluttons, these ravenous beasts will be converted to the light of the truth, or we shall all

---

[1] I see no need to enter the older discussion of the Anabaptist use or abuse of the term. For that discussion see Bainton 1936; Littell 1958; Meihuizen 1970; Hillerbrand 1971; Littell 1971; Wray 1954.

[2] Schade 1854, 347-9, 459ff.; *SB-7*, A3a-A4b; *Theodoricus* 1530, Ada; Lichtenberger, E1b-E2a; *Offenbarungen*; Osiànder, *Hildegarde* A3a-A4a.

together be plunged alive into hell.[3] The great abbott Trithemius wrote to the Emperor Maximilian I in the year 1508 that theirs was the time when iniquity had begun to take over and the love of many had grown cold.[4] Thomas Müntzer,[5] Melchior Hoffman,[6] Bernhard Rothmann,[7] Georg Fasser and Bernhard Sailer, Hutterite missionaries,[8] Peter Rideman,[9] and Menno Simons,[10] to cite only a few writers, repeated the prevalent view that the wickedness and corruption of Christendom had reached the high water mark. It could not get worse, and therefore the restitution, the great restoration, must be at hand.

In 1534 Bernhard Rothmann wrote a treatise entitled *A Restitution or Restoration of True and Sound Christian Doctrine, Faith and Living.*[11] Its purpose was to show the relationship of what had happened in Münster since the beginning of 1534 with the progress of the Reformation, but primarily with what God was doing at the end of human history to bring his purposes to pass. While what he wrote would have been rejected by many Anabaptists, his description of the times of the restitution of all things is instructive also for the rest of Anabaptism. He began with the passage from Acts 3 with which this chapter began. The restitution had begun with the renewed bright light of the gospel. This had started with the work of the scholar Martin Luther who identified the Antichrist, but who then refused to go on to complete the restitution. That would now be done by the unlearned ones. "What was begun by Erasmus, Luther, and Zwingli," he wrote, "has now been gloriously established in the truth first by Melchior [Hoffman] and Jan Matthijs and now in our brother Jan van Leiden, who are quite unlearned as the world thinks." That this was the restitution was also demonstrated by the startling fact that even as it was begun by the scholars and completed by lay people, so at the beginning the true gospel was proclaimed by lay people and corrupted by the scholars.

---

[3]Peuckert 1976, 113.

[4]Ibid., 119.

[5]Williams 1957, 49-50.

[6]*Derpten,* 262.

[7]*SBR,* 157, 215.

[8]*Hut. Ep.* I, 249.

[9]*Confession,* 151.

[10]*O.O.* 295-310; *CWMS,* 734-44.

[11]*SBR,* 219; Klaassen 1981, 332-3.

In his work *Concerning the Mystery of Scripture* Rothmann wrote that three aspects of the restitution were already in place: the true gospel was being preached, the Antichrist had been exposed, and the true church established in Münster based on repentance and baptism.[12] Before the restitution could be completed, however, everything that opposed God's plan would have to be eradicated, so that there could truly be one fold and one flock. What was begun by Christ and the Apostles would in this flock now be restored and established.[13] New hearts and spirits would mark the restitution, and justice and knowledge would be restored.[14] Then Christ would return and the End would come. Heaven and earth would be cleansed and renewed, and all would get their due reward or penalty.[15]

The overall pattern which Rothmann described there would not have been objected to by other Anabaptists, but some of the specific points were emphatically rejected. While Rothmann identified the restitution as being carried forward by Jan van Leiden's Davidic kingdom of Münster, Michael Sattler, Pilgram Marpeck, and Menno Simons saw the restitution happening in the separated, disciplined Anabaptist churches scattered across Europe. Those who wrote after its fall rejected the Münsterite vision vehemently.[16] Rothmann insisted that all opposition to God in the whole world had to be eradicated with the sword in order to present Christ with a pure church.[17] All the others except the early followers of Hut and the Davidjorists sharply repudiated that view and taught instead that the church should be kept pure by baptism of believers and the discipline of the ban.[18] It is therefore also quite consistent that Rothmann never discussed church discipline and the ban without the sword as the others did. Rather he wrote that they now lived in the kingdom of David which had been purified with the sword of righteousness and maintained by the Christian government.[19] However, and this is very important, the aim of all Anabaptists including the Münsterites was the pure

[12]Ibid., 354-5.

[13]Ibid., 218.

[14]Ibid., 356.

[15]Ibid., 358-9.

[16]See *WPM*, 209; *O.O.*, 621-31, *CWMS*, 31-50; Philips, 321-360.

[17]*SBR*, 292; Klaassen 1981, 335.

[18]*WPM*, 275-6; *O.O.*, 309-18, 337-50, 185-214; *CWMS*, 407-19, 455-86, 961-98; Philips, 390-2; Rideman, *Confession*, 131-2.

[19]*SBR*, 277-8.

church without spot or wrinkle, which would be ready for Christ when he returned. George Williams' conclusion of a quarter century ago still stands;

> The Radicals were, first of all, engaged not in a reformation of the church but, rather, in the restitution of the church. . . .[They] espoused . . .a radical rupture with the immediate past and all its institutions and [were] bent upon either the restoration of the primitive church or the assembling of a new church, all in an eschatological mood far more intense than anything to be found in normative Protestantism or Catholicism.[20]

Luther and Zwingli believed with everyone else at that time that the end was near, but that did not lead them to attempt a restitution of the true apostolic church which could be presented to Christ when he returned. They were Augustinians in their view of history. The church with its mixture of good and evil, simul justus et peccator, would exist until God's appointed End. Then Christ would return for judgment and the great eternal separation would take place. Anabaptists and others in the Radical Reformation like Thomas Müntzer and Michael Servetus belonged to another, the Joachimite view of history, which provided for the restoration of the true, purified church within history.

Several special features characterized the age of restitution. These were the belief in special reformers and prophets; the expectation of the earthly new Jerusalem, and of the earthly kingdom of Christ.

2. The Special Reformers and Prophets

Time and again we encounter in the writings of the Radical Reformation as well as in actual specific incidents the conviction that a person, especially called and anointed by God, would arise to lead the true church in the days of the End. It was usually a prophet, the returned Elijah, or in several cases, a monarch.

There are plenty of precedents for this kind of expectation. It came first in the seventh century in the form of a pious emperor who would reform the Empire at the End to prepare it for Christ's universal rule.[21] This expectation

[20]Williams 1962, 857.

[21]McGinn 1979, 75-6.

continued alive and well right into the sixteenth century.[22]   When the crisis of the church was added to that of the Empire, an angelic pope was added to the endtime expectation.   He would lead the church out of her bondage.[23] When the papacy became the Antichrist, the angelic pope became a divine prophet or a great inspired teacher.

Astronomers knew that there would be a major planetary conjunction in 1484.   Events like that invariably produced prophecies of some unusual happening.   An Italian prophecy announced the coming of a new religious leader, a monk.   When the date passed without the appearance of the promised reformer, the prophecy was modified.[24]   It was picked up by Johannes Lichtenberger.   New calculations suggested that the reformer would be born nineteen years after 1484.   This monk would preach for nineteen years and establish a new and reformed clergy.[25]   Martin Luther was born in 1483. Philip Melanchthon, his fellow-reformer, wondered whether it might in fact have been 1484.   He wanted Luther to accept a horoscope which placed his birth on 22 October, 1484.[26]   To his credit Luther rejected the proposal.   Still, many of Luther's contemporaries believed that his coming had been predicted. Zwingli and Melanchthon both referred to Luther as the returned prophet Elijah.   Did not the very last verses of the Old Testament promise that return? "Behold, I will send you Elijah the prophet before the great and terrible day of the Lord comes" (Malachi 4:5-6).   Was not this the endtime?   Had not Luther at Worms been like Elijah on Mount Carmel, only to go into hiding from his enemies after that?   Many others also referred to Luther as Elijah, and Hans Preuss claimed that Luther himself thought so.[27]   A prophecy concerning Jan Hus had by Luther's time also turned into a prediction of a new leader.   Luther accepted it as a prediction of his own coming.   "Many prophecies have gone forth, some of which refer to me."[28]   When therefore persons of the Radical Reformation assigned to themselves or others roles like that of Elijah, they had a prestigious example to follow.

[22]See *Sigismundi,* D2a-D4a; Strauss 1971, 243-6; McGinn 1979, 276.

[23]McGinn 1979, 134-5, 189-95.

[24]Warburg 1919, 37-8.

[25]Lichtenberger, O4b.

[26]Warburg 1919, 14-19.

[27]Preuss 1933, 49-51, 28-9, 30-1.

[28]Preuss 1933, 14, 17.   Preuss quotes Luther and gives specific references.   See also Clemen 1928, 402-3.

Thomas Müntzer was perceived to be a prophet. Luther regarded him as the new prophet predicted by Lichtenberger who would cause a lot of trouble.[29] His followers, among whom were Hans Hut and others, believed he was Elijah or Enoch,[30] and Müntzer proclaimed himself to be a new Daniel.[31] Hans Hut, the Anabaptist evangelist, thought of himself as John the Baptist who was also called Elijah.[32] One of his followers confessed that Hut had the book with the seven seals which the Lord had given to Daniel, and that this book would not be revealed until the Last Day.[33] Hut thus stood on the same level as Daniel. Another follower stated that once all the oppressors had been killed between Christmas 1527 and Pentecost 1528, Hut would become the endtime ruler on earth even as Christ was the ruler in heaven.[34] The coming prophet was often identified with the witnesses of Revelation 11 who would teach the ways of God or else purge the world of godlessness.[35] Others were self-proclaimed prophets like Augustin Bader and Leonhard and Ursula Jost and Barbara Rebstock of Strassburg, and many isolated instances of persons named or unnamed being identified as prophets or spirit-filled leaders.[36]

Melchior Hoffman was perhaps the most prominent of the self-announced Anabaptist prophets. His conviction that he was a prophet is clearly evident in his first major work, the commentary on Daniel XII.[37] It is clear that he identified himself with the angel of Revelation 14:6-7 who proclaimed the everlasting gospel, as well as with the angel of 10:1-7.[38] Other figures of whom he considered himself the fulfillment were the great prince Michael of Daniel 12:1,[39] and the prophet Elijah.[40] That many Anabaptists in the Netherlands and elsewhere acknowledged Hoffman as a prophet and

---

[29]Lichtenberger, N4b.

[30]Wappler, 429.

[31]Williams 1957, 64-5.

[32]*QGW* II, 60.

[33]*QGTÖ* II, 26.

[34]Wappler, 281.

[35]*TA Hesse*, 192-3; *QGW* II, 229.

[36]Röhrich 1860, 104; Wappler, 336-44; *QGW* II, 148; Grosheide I, 143.

[37]See Deppermann 1979, 58-9.

[38]*Trostliche Euangelion,* 77; *Prophecey,* B3a-b, C1b-C2a.

[39]*Prophecey,* B4a.

[40]*Romeren,* Q1b; *Sendbrieff,* 363.

particularly as Elijah is well-known.[41] When Hoffman disappeared from the Netherlands scene through his imprisonment, the prophetic mantle passed to Jan Matthijs, although not by Hoffman's decision.[42]

Even Caspar Schwenckfeld appears to have thought that he might be the special Elijah, the third one, of the endtime. This Elijah would have the special vocation of bringing together and setting right again all that was scattered and devastated in the church.[43] This description covers exactly what Schwenckfeld believed to be his vocation. The renewal of prophecy was accepted as a feature of the endtime based on Acts 2:17-18.

That men like Luther, Müntzer, Hoffman, Schwenckfeld, and even Servetus,[44] all so unlike each other, could think of themselves as actors in the drama of the endtime, indicates primarily the common powerful certainty of living at the end of time, whatever else it may say about them personally. It also demonstrates again that the sense of being oneself a fulfillment of biblical and subsequent prophecy was not limited to the people often regarded as the lunatic fringe in Reformation times.

Apart from the one reference to Hans Hut as an earthly ruler of the endtime, there were two cases of claims by specific persons to the monarchy of the Last Days. One was the claim made by Augustin Bader for his little son described in chapter III. He would be a righteous ruler once all the existing authorities in church and state had been deposed by God's elect servants. To symbolize this expectation Bader had the insignia of kingship prepared, crown, sceptre, ring, and sword. The prediction and the plan came to nothing when Bader was arrested and executed.

It was quite different in the other case, that of Jan van Leiden, who actually became king of Münster in the fall of 1534. Along with Jan Matthijs he was at first regarded as one of the prophets of Münster, and took over the leadership when Matthijs was killed in April. Jan van Leiden was 25 years old, intelligent, a talented orator, with organizational skills. He was an adventurer, having travelled considerably. He had observed, read and learned.

---

[41]Linden 1885, 231; Deppermann 1979, 179; *QGT* VIII, 13, 265; Williams 1957, 221.

[42]*Dan* I, 6; Williams 1957, 214, 220-1; Cornelius 1853, 6, 23, 29, 38-40. See Chapter III, The Age of Visionaries; van Dülmen 1974, 71-2.

[43]*CS* XIX, 349-50.

[44]Friedman 1978, 41.

There can, I believe, be no question about the genuineness of his religious convictions, nor of his ambition, and his love of pageantry and power. His reputation as prophet made it possible for him to quickly establish his position in the city. The authority of council and guilds were replaced by twelve elders chosen by him. They now oversaw the life of the city under seige. The successful fending off of two massive assaults by the besieging armies confirmed in the Münster leadership the certainty that God had chosen them as his elect to carry out his will at the End. Hence, on 8 September, Jan van Leiden was proclaimed king of the New Israel and over the whole world. He was to replace all other kings as king of righteousness and as the avenger of all injustice.[45] Now he was both prophet and king. He was seen to be a new David, a successor of the great Old Testament king, fulfilling the prediction of Jeremiah 23:5. He would occupy the throne and wield the sceptre of David until God should demand its return to him. The royal insignia were a globe pierced by silver and gold swords, the spiritual and the secular, and above them a cross with the words "The King of Righteousness Over All." The royal ring carried the same message, as did the golden chain around his neck.[46] After he was tried and condemned he was brutally tormented after the fashion of the time. A Lutheran preacher who witnessed it reported that Jan van Leiden endured the torment silently with dignity.[47] Did he, even at his bitter end try to demonstrate that he was, after all, a king?

There can be no doubt that the primary inspiration for the kingdom of Münster as the kingdom of the End was the Bible. This will be described below. Still, it does not seem far-fetched to consider the Münsterite kingdom of righteousness as an expression of the centuries-old expectation of an endtime king or emperor of righteousness whose rule would be universal after all opposition to God had been put down, and who would establish justice and peace as a prelude to the eternal kingdom of Christ. Such were the visions of *The Reformation of Sigismund*,[48] the Revolutionary of the Upper Rhine,[49] and of Wolfgang Aytinger[50] to mention only three of many. It cannot be shown that Rothmann or Jan van Leiden had read any of these prophecies. However, they were alive among ordinary people everywhere at that time.

---

[45]Cornelius 1853, 82-3.

[46]Stupperich 1983 and Detlefs 1983.

[47]van Dülmen 1974, 283.

[48]*Sigismund* I,D2a-D4a, Strauss 1971, 30-31.

[49]Strauss 1971, 244-6.

[50]McGinn 1979, 276; Rohr 1898, 44-5.

When to the popular hope and expectation we add the biblical vision of Jeremiah 23:5 which the Münsterites used, and which, along with similar images always underlay the hope for a future pious king, it is permissible to place the Münster story in that broader context. Doing that helps also to make more understandable what to so many since 1535 has appeared to be rebellion and derangement.

Still, the whole event was a kind of tragicomedy when we look back on it. While it was unfolding it need not have looked like that at all to those who were part of it. When one considers the long tradition of the coming "king of righteousness" in western Europe; when one considers further the conviction of the time that the End had come and that its particulars could be seen taking place; and when, finally, one considers the relative successes of the besieged spread over a whole year, one can muster some understanding for the Münsterite conviction that they were on the road to the realization of the kingdom of God on earth.

3. The Earthly New Jerusalem

One of the visible signs on which that conviction was based was the fact that these Anabaptists had a city. There was much more to this reality than the simple physical control of the episcopal city of Münster which had come into their hands quite legitimately. For city was not only a physical fact; it was also the product of the imagination, nurtured primarily by the image of Jerusalem, the city of God. Augustine, describing God's work and community in the world, wrote about the city of God. The borders of that city, he tells us, are invisible, but will become visible when, in the End, God is victorious over all his foes. Thus starting from the Scriptures and enlarged by Augustine, the idea of the true church as a city was well-known in the Middle Ages. Christopher Dawson alluded to this fact in his 1949 Gifford Lectures. The medieval city, he wrote, enclosed by strong walls, was a place of refuge, an oasis of security and peace in a world of turmoil.[51] The wall separated the evil outside from the virtue inside.

Already before the Reformation period there were prophecies of the importance of certain cities in the events of the End. The most prominent was Cologne, which was to be the site of the final great battle of the world. Will-Erich Peuckert tells us that there were at least 30 such prophecies, including the Kirchmair and Villingen chronicles from Tyrol as well as Johannes

---

[51]Dawson 1958, 162. See also Klaassen 1986A, 29-30.

Lichtenberger. Conrad Grebel's brother-in-law, the physician and politician Joachim von Watt also expressed this conviction basing himself on a Lollard prophecy.[52] Lichtenberger also identified Cologne as the city in which the last righteous emperor would be born. It would be a second Bethlehem, and there would be a second visit of the Three Kings bearing gifts.[53] When we therefore now look at the notion of the chosen city in Radical Reformation expectation, we are, throughout, on familiar ground.

One finds this kind of expectation in Anabaptism only in the early period of the South German and Netherlands movements. Early in 1528 an anonymous letter circulating among the followers of Hans Hut urgently advised them to be ready to travel immediately to a city which God would identify, in which they would be secure, and where they would wait for Christ's return. The writer assured them that God would give them a sign when they were to go.[54] From the same time comes a document listing eight beliefs of the Hut group. The sixth of these says that Hans Hut himself named Nicolsburg in Moravia and another named St. Gall in Switzerland as two of five cities of refuge. They did not know the names of the others.[55] The "five cities" clearly derives from Isaiah 19:18 where we read about five cities which speak the language of the land of Canaan and which have sworn allegiance to the Lord of Hosts.

In the Netherlands in the 1530s we meet with similar convictions. According to the chronicler Gresbeck the Münster prophets talked about three cities of God's chosen people in February, 1534. From these cities, Münster, Strassburg, and Deventer the new gospel would go forth into the world.[56] According to Numbers 35:14 there were to be three cities of refuge in the land of Canaan. Amsterdam Anabaptists who were interrogated about their role in the attack on the city hall in May 1535, repeated similar views. One reported that any who had not wanted to follow "the king of Münster" had been advised to go to one of three cities of refuge, Groningen, Deventer, or Amsterdam. This understanding had been given by revelation.[57] Late in 1534 word circulated among the Anabaptists of Amsterdam that Amsterdam was one of

---

[52]Peuckert 1976, 161.

[53]Kurze 1956, 332.

[54]*Sendbrieff* 1528, H2a, Isb.

[55]*QGW* II, 212.

[56]Cornelius 1853, 22-3.

[57]Grosheide I, 173, 175.

the five chosen cities which God would give to the brothers without bloodshed. The other four were Münster, Wezel, Deventer, and London.[58] The Amsterdam Anabaptists hoped it would be their city in which there would then be full equality and justice.[59] For his part, Melchior Hoffman had identified Strassburg as "the spiritual Jerusalem" in which the "banner of righteousness" would be raised up.[60] From Strassburg the gospel would go out into the whole world.[61] But when Jan Matthijs took over from Hoffman late 1533 the word was that God had cast Strassburg off because of its unbelief and had chosen Münster instead.[62] It may be of interest to add here that there were fifteenth century prophecies which identified Strassburg as the place where the last great battle of the endtime would be fought.[63]

All of this hope became a reality for some Anabaptists when they gained control of Münster early 1534. Now there was indeed a city of refuge which quickly became much more. An appeal attributed to Bernhard Rothmann was sent out from Münster in March 1534, urging Anabaptists everywhere to come to "the new Jerusalem, the city of the saints" if they wished to escape the imminent judgment of God.[64] There is some doubt that it was written by Rothmann since he never used the term "new Jerusalem" anywhere in his writings of 1534 and 1535. Nevertheless, there is no question that the Münster Anabaptists believed their city to be the new Jerusalem.[65] Several sources refer to it as the New Temple,[66] also a notion associated with the city as a religious, voluntary association in the Middle Ages.[67] The records relating to the Münster of 1534/35 as well as the writings of Bernhard Rothmann clearly reveal that the Münsterite understanding of the city was nourished chiefly by the Psalms, many of which speak of Jerusalem or Zion as God's city, God's dwelling place, from which his salvation will go forth, as well as other,

---

[58]Ibid., 12.

[59]Ibid., 12, 13, 65, 133, 136; Mellink 1954, 109, 132.

[60]*QGT* VIII, 393.

[61]Ibid., 185-6.

[62]Grosheide I, 6; Williams 1957, 133.

[63]Peuckert 1976, 159, 161.

[64]van Dülmen 1974, 78, 59.

[65]van Dülmen 1974, 81, 103, 139, 148, 185.

[66]van Dülmen 1974, 159, 182; *SBR*, 420.

[67]Dawson 1958, 163.

primarily Old Testament writings.[68] One of the best sources for what was done in the city during those months tells us that a considerable part of the school curriculum consisted of teaching the children to read and write the Psalms in German. At the beginning and end of the schoolday a Psalm was sung.[69] Rothmann specifically wrote that the Old Testament was the most important part of Scripture.[70] No doubt Jan van Leiden, who became leader in April, 1534, himself contributed much to the certainty that Münster was the new Zion by the dramatic skill which he had developed before he came to Münster.[71]

It is important that we be clear about what those Anabaptists meant when they called their city the new Jerusalem. They emphatically did not mean the New Jerusalem of Revelation 21 and 22 that came down out of heaven, the dwelling place of God with man. That was something they were still waiting for. Nor was it Augustine's city of God, that city where the just and the unjust lived together until the Great Judgment.[72] They believed that they had already made the separation and that only the just lived in Münster. Their new Jerusalem was a restitution of the faithful Jerusalem of the Psalms and Prophets. The restoration of that Jerusalem had been predicted in many places and now God had done it as a prelude to the end of history. The desolating sacrilege had been part of the old Jerusalem. Among them it had been recognized, understood, and removed. They were the renewed city of God. Their understanding of sola scriptura led them to one of its most destructive and dangerous expressions, namely the objectification of images that were meant always to remain as images and therefore as pillars of cloud and fire guiding Christians to the true city of God in and beyond time. Their view of history was not the modern one of a continuous sequence of events in a cause and effect relationship. Rather it was the medieval-Joachimite, history moving to its conclusion from one age to the next through types and their fulfillment.

The earthly historical Jerusalem was a type of the true, restored Jerusalem in Münster, finally fulfilling itself in the foursquare jewelled garden-city of Revelation. Because the original Jerusalem was a type it had to lead to its fulfillment. In the Joachimite scheme this always involved three stages

---

[68]*SBR*, 276, 285, 368-72, 373.

[69]Cornelius 1853, 47-8.

[70]*SBR*, 302, 224.

[71]van Dülmen, 1974, 151.

[72]*City of God,* 18, 54.

according to Joachim's trinitarian view of history. Something akin to that seems to have been in the minds of the Münsterite leaders.

4. The Earthly Kingdom of Christ

The expectation of a godly emperor who would set things right at the End and thus prepare the world for Christ's return naturally also included a world empire. One version of *The Reformation of Sigismund* foresaw a new Golden Age under the rule of an anointed king. At that time people would live with each other in peace, without envy or oppression. There would be enough food for all, the air would be pure, and all economic exploitation would be absent. This condition would be brought about by human decision and action.[73] The astrologer Lichtenberger also made his contributions to the expectation of this future kingdom. He hoped, he wrote, that the emperor to do it would be Maximilian I.[74] Another prophecy expected a world emperor, crowned in Rome, who would be universal ruler both secular and spiritual. He would have a long reign assuring justice, peace, and plenty.[75] A number of writers during the Reformation period, including Luther himself, wondered whether perhaps the Elector Frederick the Wise of Saxony was to be the emperor to recover the Holy Sepulchre and rule over the empire of the End which would then be surrendered to Christ at his return.[76]

In his work *Die Grosse Wende* Will-Erich Peuckert wrote that many ordinary people had no understanding for Luther's doctrine of justification by faith alone.[77] They were indeed looking for a reformation, but one which would take place with the return of the Emperor Frederick (Friedrich means man of peace) who would renew and reform the Empire, exterminate evil, and without war create the one flock under the one shepherd.[78] The yearning of ordinary people, peasants and artisans, tended to focus on the emperor as its guarantor, and to attribute the injustices under which they suffered to their immediate masters, to lawyers, financiers, and lower royal officials.[79] But

---

[73]Struve 1978, 10B.

[74]Lichtenberger, F1b-F2a.

[75]*Theodoricus* 1530, A3a-A4b.

[76]Preuss 1933, 24-5.

[77]Peuckert 1966, 606. This statement has received strong support from the newer work of Scribner 1981 and Russell 1985.

[78]Peuckert 1976, 606, 612. A specific case of this was Hans Hergot's *Neue Wandlung*.

[79]Klaassen 1978, 4-13, 30-31, for some examples.

many were disillusioned with all existing institutions and looked for something different, even to an ordinary person becoming supreme ruler.[80] This amorphous yearning was visible among some South German Anabaptists. There was talk about a new kingdom with equality. It would not be eternal but would last a very long time and would be on earth. Some believed they would themselves be in control in a society like that of the time of the Apostles. All the existing authorities would be eliminated and God would renew the world.[81] Other followers of Hut linked an earthly, divine kingdom to Christ's return to rule. The present evil world with all its pride and wealth and wisdom would be overturned so that the kingdom of heaven could be established. Christ himself would return with a glorified body for judgment to establish his kingdom, and it was emphasized over and over again that it would be established on earth in their time. They would themselves be given the task of exterminating authorities and everyone not included in their covenant.[82] Finally, they saw themselves ruling with Christ on earth. The length of that rule was indeterminate.[83] It was, all in all, a general expectation with no detailed features except those already mentioned. It was a great reversal they were expecting. They, who now suffered and died, would then be rewarded by Christ, the universal king. They would assist him in the transformation of the world and rule with him. Those who now oppressed them would be expelled from the renewed world.

There was no trace of that kind of expectation among Swiss Anabaptists, neither is it to be found in the writings of Michael Sattler or Balthasar Hubmaier. The so-called "two kingdoms" doctrine is clearly visible in the Schleitheim Articles and the other Swiss writings, but the word kingdom was rarely used, and when it was, it was in Scripture quotations. They simply used other words to describe their expectation. It may also be that Swiss political "republicanism" influenced the avoidance of kingship language, and thus saved them from going down a dangerous road.

As with the notion of the divine city that had an actual geographical location, it was Dutch Anabaptism that was drawn into kingdom expectations farthest. In 1533 Melchior Hoffman wrote that the seventh plague of Revelation 16 was about to take place. It would include the end of the

---

[80]*QGW* II, 7.

[81]*QGW* II, 61, 83, 324, 311; *TA Hesse*, 29; *QGW* II, 272; see also Klaassen 1987B.

[82]*QGW* II, 50, 51, 49, 19, 210; Wappler, 245, cf. 247.

[83]*QGW* II, 66, 37; *QGTÖ* II, 44, 116.

Babylonian and Sodomite realms. Thereafter Joseph and Solomon would come and again be rulers over the whole earth in the power of God, and thus open the way to the temple and the banquet of the Lamb.[84] Earlier he had also written about God's promise that a king from David's house would again sit on his throne. He would be Solomon, meaning Christ.[85] Although it is not altogether clear, it appears that Hoffman was looking for an earthly kingdom to be preceded by a cleansing of the earth.[86] This view of an earthly kingdom can also be found among Hoffman's followers in the Netherlands.[87]

No wonder then, that it also found its way to Münster in 1534. In fact, that is where the view of an earthly kingdom of Christ was most fully developed. It was part of the expectation related to the new Jerusalem and the kingship of Jan van Leiden which began in September, 1534. When he was made king it was not only over the new Israel of Münster but over the whole world. He would displace all other authorities as king of righteousness and would punish all injustice and wickedness in the world.[88] These are formulations virtually identical with those of the late Middle Ages, and some of them doubtless came from Jan van Leiden himself. It is quite possible that he was familiar with plays about the Last World Emperor since he had earlier participated in theatrical productions.[89]

It was Bernhard Rothmann who rationalized the conviction about Christ's earthly reign in his works *The Restitution* and *Concerning Vengeance*. In the end Christ's kingdom would be extended over the whole world. But the devil had ejected Christ from his rightful kingship immediately after the time of the Apostles and had usurped it himself. Hence the kingdom had begun spiritually, having been prevented by the devil from being fully revealed in power on earth. But with the help of his servants Christ would defeat the devil and all ungodliness and reclaim his kingdom and reign.[90] He would rule on earth

---

[84]*Unterrichtung*, A2b.

[85]*Weyssagung*, D2a; *Romeren*, X6a-b.

[86]See also Deppermann 1979, 297-8.

[87]Grosheide I, 81; Meihuizen 1954, 45.

[88]Cornelius 1853, 82-3.

[89]See Cornelius 1853, 168, which is a description of a drama in the cathedral which the king himself supervised. See Zeschwitz 1881.

[90]*SBR*, 272.

until all his enemies were defeated. Then he would surrender the kingdom to God.[91]

To initiate this restitution God had fulfilled the old promise to restore the Davidic monarchy (Jeremiah 23:5) in the kingship of Jan van Leiden.[92] He was the third David, and Christ was Solomon. David's kingdom had been one of vengeance and wrath, and of gathering what was necessary for the building of the temple. Then came Solomon who reigned in peace and built the temple. Those images were now fulfilled in the new David who was preparing for the kingdom of the coming peaceful Solomon by exterminating all injustice,[93] and by cleansing the world with the sword of justice.[94] All of this had been confirmed by miracles.[95] Soon there would be one fold and one flock and one king over all. All creatures would be liberated. God's pure obedient people would inherit the earth and be the servants of Christ the king over all. This, he kept repeating, will happen in this time on earth.[96] He appealed to people around Münster and in the Netherlands to come to Münster, to rally to "the banner of righteousness," and fight with David to prepare for the peaceful kingdom of Christ.[97]

The Münsterite kingship of Jan van Leiden was therefore really preparation for the rule of Christ, a visible prelude or prologue to the peaceable kingdom which would begin only with the return of Christ to earth.

Whereas the use of the kingdom concept was unknown in Swiss Anabaptism, it was widely used by Anabaptist writers after Münster. Especially Menno Simons and Dirk Philips were forced to clarify the proper understanding of the term for north European Anabaptists. Because they were charged with the Münsterite errors,[98] Menno found himself explaining again and again that he and his churches held a different view of the kingdom of Christ than the Münsterites. He totally rejected the Münsterite claims for Jan

---

[91]*SBR*, 273.

[92]*SBR*, 294; Cornelius 1853, 277; van Dülmen 1974, 149.

[93]*SBR*, 295.

[94]*SBR*, 278.

[95]*SBR* 279, 282.

[96]*SBR*, 279, 282.

[97]*SBR*, 273.

[98]*SBR*, 296-7, 290.

van Leiden's Davidic kingship and confessed that Jesus was the only true king.[99] He never varied from the basic position he expressed in *The Foundation of Christian Doctrine* in 1539:

> The kingdom of Christ is not of this visible, tangible, transitory world, but . . . is an eternal, spiritual, and abiding kingdom which is not eating and drinking, but righteousness, peace, and joy in the Holy Ghost. In it no king reigns except the true King of Zion, Christ Jesus. He is the King of righteousness, the King of kings, who has all power in heaven above, and on earth beneath, before whom every knee must bow and all tongues praise. The true king David in the Spirit who through his righteousness, merits and crimson blood has delivered the sheep from the mouth of the hellish lions and bears, has slain the great and terrible Goliath, and obtained for the spiritual Israel of God eternal welfare and peace. Neither this King or his servants bear any sword but the sword of the Spirit. . . . With the Word of God . . . he defends the kingdom against the gates of hell, and graciously keeps and guards its supremacy in the midst of heavy cross and trial. And this he does not with iron or steel . . . for His kingdom and dominion is spirit and not letter.[100]

He did not hesitate to use the Psalms Rothmann used, but he interpreted them spiritually.[101] He referred to Jesus as the true Solomon who sits on the eternal throne of David, but who receives his kingdom not from an earthly king, but from God.[102] He rejected with horror Rothmann's teaching that Christians were the instruments of God's vengeance, and that such vengeance should take place before Christ's return.[103] The kingdom of Christ is only and always a kingdom of peace and so are the weapons used in it.[104] The kingdom of Christ is the church,[105] or at least it is the visible form of that kingdom.[106] This kingdom is real and visible in this world to the extent that

---

[99]*O.O.*, 64-70; *CWMS*, 199, 215-221.

[100]*O.O.*, 65; *CWMS*, 217.

[101]*O.O.*, 622, 627; *CWMS*, 35, 44.

[102]*O.O.*, 56; *CWMS*, 199.

[103]*O.O.*, 629; *CWMS*, 46-7.

[104]*O.O.*, 502, 126, 55; *CWMS*, 554-5, 94, 198.

[105]*O.O.*, 502, *CWMS*, 554, 1031.

[106]Meihuizen I, 47.

Christians are obedient and conform to the teachings and example of Christ, their king.

Dirk Philips also refuted the Münsterite view of the restitution of the Davidic kingdom in Münster. In 1560 he wrote his *Spiritual Restitution.* He argues that Jesus was the spiritual fulfillment of the physical David as well as of the peaceful Solomon. He built the spiritual temple, the church. In it also was restored spiritually the great glory and wisdom of Solomon. In this church were also the twelve rulers, namely the twelve apostles, his parallel to the Twelve Dukes of Münster.[107] He continued by explaining the history of Israel in detail, showing how it was all spiritually restored in Christ.[108] The kingdom of Christ was therefore not something to wait for; it was already here, but it was internal and spiritual, a position not unlike that of Augustine. For both Menno and Dirk the believers work with Christ to defeat evil and the devil.[109] They attempted a point by point refutation of Münster. What they created was a negative image of Münster and so did not really separate themselves from it.

Others in the Radical Reformation spiritualized the kingdom of Christ to such an extent that, like Hans Denck, they were very reluctant to accord it outward form, or completely rejected any visible form of the church as Schwenckfeld and Franck did. Pilgram Marpeck rarely used the notion of kingdom, perhaps again to avoid the problems inherent in it. He dealt extensively with the nature and role of the church but preferred these other images well before Münster which means that his post-Münster writings were not determined by that event even though he was very much aware of it.[110]

All Anabaptists believed that they lived at the End of time, and all held to some version of the restitution, the re-establishment in their time and place of the church as God wanted it to be, modelled on the Bible. All believed that God was at work guiding the events of their time to his End. All believed that they were participants with God who had put themselves voluntarily and deliberately at God's disposal through baptism and the surrender to the guidance of the Holy Spirit.

[107]Cornelius 1853, 179-88.

[108]Philips, 348-63.

[109]Meihuizen I, 45.

[110]See *WPM*, 209; *Aufdeckung,* B4a; Klassen 1968, 138, 142.

The precise nature of their participation varied, however, For most it consisted chiefly in being obedient followers of Jesus, in submitting themselves to the discipline of the church, keeping it pure for the Bridegroom's return, and witnessing to the truth of the gospel. For others it meant assisting God in establishing his sovereignty on earth in a visible, tangible way.

Both approaches could be justified from the Scriptures; it depended on how they were interpreted. Certainly the new emphasis of the Reformation on a literal reading of Scripture contributed much to what happened in Anabaptism, in Münster no less than in Zürich. The Münsterites were as much children of the Reformation and of the Anabaptist movement as the Swiss Brethren and the later Mennonites. The issues in biblical interpretation which produced such variety in Anabaptists eschatological expectation even today show no signs of being resolved.

VI. The Age of the Spirit

On the morning of Easter in the year 1183 the abbot Joachim of Fiore had a vision in which the entire harmony of the Old and New Testaments was revealed to him with great clarity. A second vision shortly afterwards on the day of Pentecost gave him a revelation of the Holy Trinity.[1] From these revelations Joachim concluded that history unfolded according to a trinitarian scheme of three ages, the ages of the Father, the Son, and the Holy Spirit. The age of the Father had lasted until the birth of Christ, the age of the Son was about to end, and the age of the Spirit would soon commence. God's revelation had become clearer as time progressed, and would achieve ultimate clarity in the last age. In that last age of the Spirit all the impediments to perceiving and understanding God's will would be overcome and God would reveal himself directly to all. Old Testament prophecy was entirely clear on this point:

> This is the covenant I will make with the house of Israel after those days, says the Lord: I will put my law within them, and I will write it upon their hearts; and I will be their God, and they shall be my people. And no longer shall each man teach his neighbour and each his brother saying, 'Know the Lord,' for they shall all know me, from the least of them to the greatest, says the Lord (Jeremiah 31:33-4).[2]

This tripartite scheme of history showed up repeatedly after Joachim and on into the sixteenth century,[3] sometimes clearly as in Hans Hergot, or less obviously as in Bernhard Rothmann, who wrote about "three worlds" the second of which was now coming to an end.[4] The whole of the Radical Reformation was united in the view that they were living in the endtime and that the most important feature of their time was a renewed outpouring of the Holy Spirit. They believed that they were living in the time of the Spirit. No one appealed to Joachim for this belief, but, like Joachim, they all appealed to the Scriptures. An obvious passage was Acts 2:17-18:

---

[1]McGinn 1985, 21-2. McGinn also provides the Latin original in the notes.

[2]For a recent discussion of Joachim's system see McGinn 1985, 99-203.

[3]Reeves 1976, 136-65.

[4]*SBR*, 332-3, 347-8; Vogler 1988, 106-7.

And in the last days it shall be, God declares, that I will pour out my Spirit upon all flesh, and your sons and your daughters shall prophesy, and your young men shall see visions, and your old men shall dream dreams; yea, and on my menservants and my maidservants in those days I will pour out my Spirit; and they shall prophesy.

Because they believed themselves to be living in the age of the Spirit, it was quite natural that these people should claim that the Spirit revealed the truth to them directly, that visions were a medium of revelation, that the Spirit opposed the scholars with their worldly methods of interpreting Scripture, and follow the call to perfection, the total sanctification of the believer and the church by the Holy Spirit.

1.   Appeal to the Spirit

In the early 1520s the late medieval stream of anticlerical piety had a brief flirtation with the new teaching coming from Wittenberg. Almost singlehanded Luther had wrested religious authority from the clerics of the church of Rome and vested it in the Scriptures. The Bible was an authority to which even lay people had direct access. Vernacular translations were available in printed form before Luther's translation appeared.[5] All that was required, therefore, to bypass clerical control was access to a Bible and someone to read it. In 1520 determined people could manage that. Whatever else Luther had done since late 1517, he had created among people a sense of freedom to take into their own hands what had traditionally been the preserve of the clergy,[6] and people were not slow to do it. This readiness on the part of lay people prompted the Fifth Lateran Council to decree on 19 December, 1516, that anyone who made predictions of the future and the Antichrist, even when based on Scripture, without first submitting it in advance to the papal censors, would be subject to sanctions.[7]

There were stirrings everywhere, people speaking out as partisans of the "new Hercules" as Luther was called, who laid about him with his cudgel to the delight of his countrymen. One such place was Zwickau, a Saxon town, about 75 miles south of Wittenberg, where Thomas Müntzer had spent time in

---

[5]Lockwood 1969, 433-6.

[6]For an excellent treatment of this phenomenon see Goertz 1987, 52-90.

[7]Preuss 1933, 21.

1520-21. When he published his call for reformation in the so-called Prague Manifesto on 25 November, 1521, he sounded a new note not hitherto heard in quite that resonance and intensity. It was a passionate, eloquent, thundering challenge to the clerical church. He introduced his manifesto as the "new" praise song of the Holy Spirit, as if to say, "The new age has begun. The yeast is making the dough climb out of the bowl. The new wine is bursting the old wineskins and producing excitement and joy all around." Every Christian, in order to hear and understand God, now required the sevenfold spirit of God (Isaiah 11:2-3). He kept repeating that the seventh gift, the spirit of the fear of God, was what was now required in this time of the End. The twelfth century bishop Gerhoh von Reichersberg had divided Christian history according to the seven gifts of the Spirit. His time, he believed, was the age of the sixth gift. The seventh, the spirit of the fear of the Lord, would come in the endtime.[8] According to Müntzer, this time had now come. All true preachers of the gospel would now need to have revelations inspired by the Spirit in order to preach with authority. Scripture alone would not do because, as had happened for so long, it could be thrown to the people in pieces as one throws food to a dog or as the storks regurgitate raw frogs to their young. The clerics argued that God no longer spoke person to person as in biblical times. But this, replied Müntzer, was the new time of the Spirit and so it was happening again. And this speaking of God in the Spirit was, Müntzer repeated over and over again, opposed to the view that he spoke only through the Scriptures. The human heart was the parchment on which God wrote the true holy Scriptures with his living finger, and it was to this process that the whole of the written Scriptures testified. This true Scripture, assured Müntzer, could be read by all of God's elect. For this one did not need to be literate. He would, he promised, put the clerics to shame in the Spirit of Elijah.[9] In these ten pages Müntzer touched on most of the major current themes regarding the age of the Spirit. The reference to Elijah calls for some explanation. As already described earlier, Elijah the prophet was expected to return at the End according to Malachi 4:5. Elijah had come to be identified in a special way with the spirit of prophecy. He typified the Holy Spirit. He had been taken bodily into heaven where he had learned the secrets of God's purposes. When he returned he would reveal them so that everyone would turn to God and be saved. But Elijah was also an active prophet. It was he who had killed the 400 prophets of Baal on Mt. Carmel in order to cleanse Israel from its idolatry. When Müntzer promised to put the clerics (read prophets of

---

[8]Meuthen 1959, 126-7.

[9]*TMSB*, 495-505.

Baal) to shame in the spirit of Elijah, he was making a threat which his listeners could not have missed. The main point, however, was that God spoke now, in this time, to any person, no matter how lowly, who was waiting to hear God's voice. God interposed nothing between himself and the listener, no clerics and no Bible.

This was the message that Philip Melanchthon, the young professor at Wittenberg University, heard on 27 December, 1521, from three men who had come from Zwickau to see him. Their visit was not a casual one. They had come to announce the new time of the Spirit to the leaders in Wittenberg in the hope that they would accept it and take the Reformation to its consummation. All three of them were laymen. They claimed that they had been called to teach by the clear, ringing voice of God, and that God alone told them what and where to speak. They raised questions about infant baptism since the children could not produce the faith which was a requirement for baptism. The three claimed also to have knowledge of the future and called themselves prophetic and apostolic.[10] They were picking up where the Apostles had left off. They were clearly restitutionists, and part of that was a new equipment with the Holy Spirit. Like the men and women of old they "spoke as they were moved by the Holy Spirit." Melanchthon was very disturbed. He was impressed and yet again uneasy. Were these the lay people who would interpret Scripture and understand it as Luther had hoped? Were these the people who could be independent of the clerics and scholars and make the judgments required of Christian people? Nicholas Amsdorf, a Wittenberg cleric, said that he regarded their coming as a sign of the End. However, caution and suspicion triumphed, and the Zwickau Prophets, as Luther called them, left no influence on Wittenberg. Luther said they were crazy.

As we know, Müntzer was executed in 1525, and the Prophets disappeared well before then.[11] But others were ready to take their place, especially among the Anabaptists. For Anabaptists were, all of them, Spirit people. Appeal to inspiration by God's Spirit has often, in the history of the church, been made by those who were not Scripture scholars as a way of legitimizing their interpretation and understanding of Scripture. But in the case of Anabaptism there was also the conviction of living in the endtimes in which a new outpouring of the Spirit would take place. Hence we are told by

[10]Wappler 1966, 58-9.

[11]However, see the report on Storch in the Chronicle of Enoch Widmann in *QGW* II, 4-10.

Anabaptists in and around Zürich in the first years that they did what they did by direction of God's Spirit.[12]

Like the Swiss Brethren, Anabaptists in South Germany also saw themselves as immediately inspired and guided by the Holy Spirit. These people (and the Münsterites) were the Pentecostalists of the sixteenth century. They came in the wake of the views and activity of Thomas Müntzer through his disciple Hans Hut. Their views on Spirit-inspiration came not quite as directly from the reading of the Gospels as with the humanist-influenced Anabaptists of Zürich. The main source of South German Anabaptism was medieval mysticism which taught that God spoke directly to the human soul. And Scripture, as they read it, confirmed that view. The Bible was full of stories in which God spoke directly to people without any intermediary agency. He spoke to Abraham, to Daniel, to Peter and Paul. They heard his voice and responded. And these Anabaptists believed that God still did it, especially in these Last Days. This conviction was a Godsend for ordinary people because they were now no longer shut out of communion with God by clerics they could not trust and a Bible most of them could not read. Hans Denck, writing with fiery conviction, said: "Whoever cannot read, let him go in self-surrender to the Master who is the schoolmaster of all the doctors. He alone has the key to this book [of the Scriptures] in which all the treasures of wisdom are enclosed."[13] It came as a wonderful liberation and established their status as enfranchised, mature children of God, and as his ennobled witnesses.[14]

Take the case of Georg Nespitzer. He had been baptized and appointed as a preacher and baptizer by Hans Hut. In 1529 he sent two letters to Anabaptists under his care. He was himself probably illiterate since he identified the writer of one of the letters. God, he wrote, had given them the Spirit in their hearts and set the divine seal on their foreheads. The time of preaching to others was over (No man will teach his brother . . .), for all now had to be taught by God himself. But God would reveal himself and speak only to those who were worthy of it.[15] Another case, slightly more exotic, was that of Jörg Lenglein. He rejected the Lutheran teaching regarding the sacrament and said that he had been commissioned so to teach by Christ

---

[12]*QGTS* I, 65, 223; *QGW* II, 246, and many more. I assembled the evidence in my Oxford dissertation "Word, Spirit, and Scripture in Early Anabaptist Thought", 1960.

[13]*DS*, 74.

[14]*GZ* I, 70-3.

[15]*QGW* II, 168-70; cf. 68.

through the Spirit. He had, he said, prayed for the Spirit, and had been taught and converted and led by that Spirit. And then he went on in his confession to describe prophetic visions he had had of a huge worm set to attack the city of Nuremberg.[16] We should not allow such claims to folk-tale revelations to obscure the main point of Lenglein's confession which was his sense of being in on God's counsels through the Spirit. Georg Gross Pfersfelder was a member of the lower nobility who came to the defence of Anabaptists and other dissenters. He expressed a conviction they all shared that

> God the Father now, in these last times, again works mightily among the lowly and simple through his Holy Spirit as he did in the beginning when Christ was on earth. He again teaches the unlearned his divine way of salvation.[17]

He admitted that there may at times be false people among them as was the case, he slyly implied, also with the Lutherans. He was referring to the so-called Dreamers of Uttenreuth, who had drifted into an uncontrolled living in the Spirit which included the disappearance of traditional sexual restraints,[18] a phenomenon known elsewhere in Christian history.[19] It was, however, relatively uncommon in the Radical Reformation.

Melchior Hoffman, the father of Dutch Anabaptism, believed himself to be especially gifted with the Holy Spirit. He took great pride in the fact that he was an ordinary man (he was a furrier by profession) and not a cleric,[20] since it was to the simple that God was revealing himself. The wisdom of God, so long hidden, was now being poured over all flesh. All of God's children, not only the clergy and doctors, were anointed and sealed with the Holy Spirit. The young were now speaking in the Spirit as Joel had said. The words of Mary were fulfilled: "He has filled the hungry with good things and has sent the rich away empty." *Those who can't read do understand: those who can, don't.*[21] God is no respecter of persons when he distributes the exalted gifts of the Holy Spirit. They are given to all who believe him, but

---

[16]*QGW* II, 349.

[17]*QGW* II, 231; Friesen & Klaassen 1982, 51.

[18]*QGW* II, 318-23.

[19]There were, for example, the Brethren of the Free Spirit in earlier centuries. Russell 1971, 86-91.

[20]*Amsdorf,* B1a.

[21]*Daniel XII,* D3b-D4a. Author's emphasis.

especially to the poor, whom, unlike the powerful of the earth, God does not despise.[22] It was not until 1534 that Hoffman explicitly referred to himself as Elijah, the Spirit-prophet returned.[23] But he had hinted at it ever since his Daniel commentary in 1526.[24] In 1530 he pointed to a strong teacher in God's Spirit and knowledge who went into heaven where he was in the school of God and had now returned (Rev. 10:1).[25] This appears to be a reference to Elijah with whom he had specifically compared himself.[26]

2. Appeal to Visions

The whole Anabaptist movement believed itself to be under the immediate inspiration of God. One of the mediums for divine communication in the Spirit age was visions. They were specifically predicted for the endtimes. It is therefore not surprising that many Anabaptists had visions. Did not the Bible record many instances of visions given by God to his servants? Conrad Grebel, Georg Blaurock, and Felix Mantz were all said to have had visions.[27] The epistolary letter written by a follower of Hans Hut reported repeated visions by the author, the main function of which seem to have been to underscore the urgency of faithfulness in the few remaining days before the End.[28] The report of a vision given to an imprisoned Anabaptist was obviously influenced by the miraculous prison escape of Peter in Acts 12:6-17.[29] Visions were especially plentiful in Strassburg in Hoffman's circle. Hoffman published a whole book of the visions of Ursula Jost.[30] These have often been identified as the pathological ravings of disturbed minds. Hoffman's most recent biographer called them "the reflexes of an unusually sensitive medium" who translated the hopes and fears of her surroundings into fantastic images,[31] in some ways reminiscent of the visions of Hildegard von

---

[22]*Offenbarung*, A3b-A4a.

[23]*QGT* VIII, 386.

[24]*Daniel XII*, A2b.

[25]*Offenbarung*, L7b-L8a. Cf. Z1b.

[26]*Dialogus*, C3b-C4a.

[27]*QGTS* I, 123, 125, 215, 217.

[28]*Sendbrieff*, E1b, E4a, G2b, G3a, H2a-b, J3a, J4b-K1a.

[29]*QGW* II, 169.

[30]*Gesicht*.

[31]Deppermann 1979, 181.

Bingen.[32] These visions greatly influenced events in the Netherlands after 1530 where they had more acclaim than among Hoffman's followers in Strassburg.[33] There too, people had visions in a tense apocalyptic atmosphere.[34]

Rothmann reported similar occurrences in Münster. Every major decision made there was supported by appeal to divine instructions and visions. Rothmann accepted visions as evidences that the Münsterites were on the right track and that God was with them.[35] Discussion as to whether people actually had those visions is beside the point here. Visions were predicted for the age of the Spirit in the Scriptures, and therefore many people, who were certain that they were living in that age, would regard them as real. Certainly they were real to the extent that they influenced their decisions.

3. Appeal to the Spirit against the Scholars

Visions and revelations given by the Spirit were for the most part limited to lay people who used them as a counterweight to the claims of scholars, hierarchs, and clergy to be the mediators of God's message. The conviction that ordinary, even illiterate, lay people could understand God's message better than the scholars had grown to explosive potential throughout the late Middle Ages. It is a view that can be traced back at least to the Waldensians in the late twelfth century.[36] It is very evident in *The Reformation of Sigismund* of the mid-fifteenth century.[37] This work loosely quotes Matthew 11:25: "Almighty God, you have most often concealed your wisdom from the wise of this world and have revealed it to the little people."[38] Popular pamphlets of the early Reformation invariably juxtaposed the simple and the learned. They pointed to the fact that the birth of Christ was revealed first to simple shepherds, and that Christ had chosen very ordinary simple people as his disciples. Sebastian Lotzer, a leader in raising the consciousness of the dignity of lay people, wrote in 1523:

---

[32]*Scivias*, 1986.

[33]Deppermann 1979, 181.

[34]Grosheide I, 12, 48-9, 100.

[35]*SBR*, 280-1.

[36]Lambert 1977, 78.

[37]*Sigismundi*, D2a.

[38]Ibid., A4b.

For the sake of your souls' salvation, have a care for the wolves who say that laymen have no right to read the Bible because they don't understand it. It's a lie! God Almighty has always given and never begrudged his divine word to the simple, godly, honest people. When he was about to be born, he announced it to shepherds, not to the Scripture-wizards and pharisees.[39]

The humanist view of Philip Melanchthon that the carriers of history were the great ones, and that ordinary people had no part in the process, was shared by many educated people.[40] But Luther had given ordinary people a sense of dignity and it bore fruit even though they soon included him with the apostate scholars.

There was virtual unanimity among Anabaptists, as Hans Hergot said, "that God the Holy Spirit gives more wisdom to an . . . unlearned man than to a[n] . . . educated one."[41] Lay people equipped with the Holy Spirit over against clerical scholars with sacramental ordination and the devices of scholarship: it was an explosive notion that made lay people into God's elect children of the Last Days, and made the clerical scholars into partisans of the Antichrist. Hans Hut called the universities of Wittenberg and Paris dens of murder and knavery where it was impossible to learn the secret of divine wisdom. But it would be learned among the poor, the despised of the world who are called crazies and devils.[42] To think that one could learn these mysteries in the schools was putting the cart before the horse or like trying to learn a craft like goldsmithing from a verbal description, wrote the former Franciscan Leonhard Schiemer.[43] When Melchior Hoffman was preaching in Dorpat in what is today the Soviet republic of Esthonia, his credibility was attacked by the Lutheran clergy because he was a layman and a furrier who did not have the training to interpret Scripture. True authority, responded Hoffman, did not reside in such scholarship. If anyone desires that authority, it must be acquired from God who gives to those who ask.[44] He could have been with the Lutherans and Zwinglians and in kings' palaces, he wrote in 1532. He had actually been there so it was not empty boasting. But the price of such fame, he wrote,

---

[39]Russell 1983, 128-9.

[40]Mencke-Glückert 1912, 53-4.

[41]Steinmetz 1977, B4b. Cf. *QGW* II, 244.

[42]*GZ* I, 14.

[43]*GZ* I, 74.

[44]*Daniel XII*, N3a.

would have been to have a double heart, to be two-faced. So he had chosen to abandon the worldly wise and powerful to sit in the mud with God's poor, lowly, believing children. He would rather be a prophecy-freak than a scholar.[45] For scholars tended to act against the truth with their scholarship, and with it to murder innocent blood.[46] In Münster, wrote Bernhard Rothmann, God had restored gloriously through the simple and uneducated what had earlier been devastated by the scholars.[47] In his last writing he angrily attacked the Augsburg Reformer Urban Rhegius who had belittled Rothmann for his lack of scholarship. So be it, he wrote. "I am an uneducated grammarian and know nothing about dialectics, but he is the famous Superior Doctor who is able to turn out clever syllogisms and cunning fictions .... God, who is a just judge be thanked. We will leave to him to determine who sinks or swims."[48] Rothmann had no doubt that God would decide for the poor grammarian with the Spirit and against the famous Superior Doctor with his spiritless scholarship.

Even the later and more reflective Anabaptist leaders echoed these sentiments:

> God entrusts his truth to the faithful and truly innocent ones, but conceals it from the learned, wise, sly, and obstinately independent. He reveals it to the simple, uneducated, course, faithful people, who witness to the truth with poor, course, simple words and speech . . . .
> Therefore to learn the language of the simple, faithful, truly believing hearts is now, in these last dangerous times, when the fullness of the Gentiles has come in, a thousand times more necessary and useful than to learn Latin, Greek, Hebrew or other languages.[49]

So wrote Pilgram Marpeck in 1544. Now that the End was near, the message of the simple believers carried more weight than that of the scholars. When Menno Simons wrote about the perversions of the simple gospel by the scholars, he resorted invariably to apocalyptic language.[50] Their work was a

---

[45]*Majestät,* A2a-b.

[46]*Romeren,* X3a. Cf. *Romeren,* C5a; *Das . . . Trostliche euangelion,* 78.

[47]*SBR,* 219.

[48]*SBR,* 398. Cf. 249, 338, 343, 363.

[49]*WPM,* 370-1. Cf. *Aufdeckung,* A3a.

[50]*O.O.,* 444, 607, 618; *CWMS,* 303, 927, 943.

sign of the End as also was the Spirit-inspired obedient faith of the simple people.

The early period of Anabaptism in all three major areas was charismatic in nature, more so in South Germany and the Netherlands than in Switzerland. With the emphasis on the immediate inspiration of the Spirit came also varying degrees of ignoring and even despising of traditional constraints within which and marks by which claims to Spirit guidance could be judged. Many Anabaptists rejected those precisely because they were associated with all the abuses from which they had separated themselves. Later writers, most notably Pilgram Marpeck and Menno Simons, returned to safer ground which could more adequately serve and preserve their congregations of believers. The Spirit works through the external services of the church, through church order and the sacraments, and the various experiences of the Christian life, but even so not in a predictable, invariable way. The Spirit is not capricious, but can also not be domesticated.[51] Menno Simons, writing in 1550, produced a thoroughly orthodox statement on the Holy Spirit. He desperately needed to dissociate himself and his churches from the taint of Münster.[52]

The conviction that God revealed himself to the simple and unlettered as well as to the scholars, amounted to a democratization of revelation.[53] It was a lay theology that logically went with the priesthood of all believers. Nor was it a rejection of scholarship as such, since Grebel, Mantz, Hubmaier, Sattler, Marpeck, Rothmann, Menno and a good many other Anabaptists in the early period had scholarly training. But unless that scholarship was put into the service of faithfulness and obedience in the short time that remained before Christ's return, it became a servant of the Antichrist. The test of a correct interpretation of the Bible was not sufficient and acknowledged scholarly equipment and skill, but was quite simply obedience.[54] Only as Jesus' example and teaching was followed would one know whether it was true. Obedience was the only qualification required for correct interpretation and understanding of the Scriptures.[55]

[51]*WPM*, 453-4; 505. See also Klaassen 1978A.

[52]*O.O.*, 398-90; *CWMS*, 495-6.

[53]See Ozment 1973, 105.

[54]*GZ* II, 46-7.

[55]See articles 1-4 Swartley 1984.

4. The Call to Perfection

That brings us to the last major aspect of the Age of the Spirit. Part of the restitution which the people of the Radical Reformation saw taking place was the restoration of a life of obedience to Christ. The Acts 3 passage specifically stated that they were to listen to this prophet whom God would send in whatever he told them. The prophet was Jesus, and they were determined to listen to him. Purity in the life of the individual believer and the purity of the church were the conditions for being the true church of the endtime. Only a pure church could hope to be acceptable to Christ when he returned.

a. Personal holiness

For Anabaptism this striving to listen to Jesus and doing what he said has been called discipleship although the term was never used by them. Still, that is what it was. They believed they were called to follow in the footsteps of Jesus and the example he left them.[56] However, this was not merely an external following of certain rules. Fundamentally it represented a belief that those who truly followed were in that process made over, transformed into Jesus' likeness, so that one began to act and speak like Jesus.[57] It was the process of personal sanctification. Baptism was the door by which the believers entered into holiness; by it they were totally cleansed, wrote Pilgram Marpeck.[58] Every disciple who persevered in the trials and tribulations of the endtimes would participate in the Great Supper of the Lamb (Rev. 3:20).[59] That perseverance was possible only with the help of God; no Anabaptist ever thought that it was possible to live the holy life in one's own strength. At the same time the writings are full of admonitions and imperatives to live the holy life, with constant reminders that if one failed there would be no admission to the Great Supper. "Although thou art pure, make thyself holier still; although thou art righteous, make thyself more righteous still . . . Let your whole body be pure and immaculate, for thy lover hates all wrinkles and spots.[60] The holy city of God will not tolerate anything unclean! Along with the promise of God's help there was, therefore, also a very strong motivation for human effort to make sure the prize was not missed. It was a fearful position to be

---

[56]*QGTS* I, 219; *QGW* II, 70; *GZ* I, 89; *DS*, 45, 50; *SBR*, 236, 317.

[57]*DS*, 53, 84.

[58]*WPM*, 200-01.

[59]*GZ* II, 47.

[60]*O.O.*, 67; *CWMS*, 221.

in. Melchior Hoffman drew on 4 [2] Esdras 7 to dramatize it. The road to the city of God runs over a path only one foot wide. On the right is fire, on the left water. Whoever could not get across would be damned and forever excluded from the city.[61] The image put enormous weight on human effort. The disciple kept fighting the sin until the battle was won and there was peace.[62] Only believers who were purified, sanctified, or to use Hans Denck's word, deified, could hope to meet the Bridegroom when he came.[63] In fact, the matter of purity in the face of the return of Christ was so crucial that, as Melchior Hoffman and Bernhard Rothmann taught, there could be no forgiveness for deliberate sins, no matter how small, for a believer who had once been regenerated.[64] This view was not shared by other Anabaptists.[65] The perfectionist strain with its unyielding rigour was also strongest in Dutch Anabaptism where apocalyptic expectation was highest. Hoffman came very close to complete perfectionism in his commentary on Romans. True believers were Christians whose feet no longer slipped, who could no longer sin, who already ruled with Christ, and who were prisoners of the Holy Spirit.[66] In the circle of Marpeck churches, where the holiness motif was also strong, much more account was taken of the ongoing potential for sin in the believer accompanied by a much more patient and gentle church discipline than that exercised among Swiss and Dutch.[67]

b. The purity of the church

But perfection was also the mark of the church, the whole company of believers, not only of the individual believer. The Bride of Christ (2 Cor. 11:2, Eph. 5:27) was a favourite image for the church among Anabaptists. The Swiss used it only rarely, not at all in the beginning, and only a few times later.[68] Among the South German Anabaptists it was common. Among the Dutch, Menno Simons used the image virtually every time he described the church. The church, brought into being by the work of Jesus on the cross and

---

[61]*Unterrichtung,* A6a. Cf. Yoder 1973, 116 and *O.O.,* 166; *CWMS,* 68.

[62]*GZ* I, 217-18.

[63]*DS,* 39; *Daniel XII,* H2b.

[64]*Unterrichtung,* A4a, A5a; *Judas,* A7b-A8b, B6b-B7a, C1a; *SBR,* 233, 255, 278.

[65]An exception was Ulrich Stadler in *GZ* I, 216.

[66]*Romeren,* L1a-b, P6b. Cf. *QGT* IV, 254; *QGTÖ* II, 132, 335; *QGTÖ* III, 151.

[67]See Klaassen 1978A.

[68]*QGTS* II, 151; *QGTS* IV, 317.

the continuing work of the Holy Spirit, was, because it was God's creation, pure, without spot or wrinkle, holy and without blemish. It was the new Eve, the congregation of God which had been cleansed and purified by God of all uncleanness. Only so could she appear without shame at the Wedding Feast.[69] While it is important to remember always about this Anabaptist view of the church that she was pure in the first instance because she was the creation of God, and not neglect to notice the clear recognition by virtually all that sin continued to work in her life,[70] there was immense pressure also to take specific human action to ensure her actual purity. The Schleitheim doctrine of separation was a first expression of the urgency of this within Anabaptism, and already then was clearly set in the context of the nearness of Christ's return. They were to make every effort to keep the church pure until his coming. That coming was a matter of a short time only.[71] This point was also made strongly by Michael Sattler in his letter to Horb.[72] For this reason also Menno rejected the Protestant interpretation of the Parable of the Tares which was that good and bad should remain together in the church until God would separate them in the Last Judgment. The church, countered Menno, was required to be pure now.[73] Pilgram Marpeck concurred with that view. The holy church could be built only with believers. No one could belong who did not have holiness and love.[74] All who did not meet those qualifications were excluded with the ban.[75] Marpeck was confident also that the baptism of adult believers would ensure the holiness of the church.[76]

While, as pointed out earlier, the Münsterites never discussed church discipline with the ban, they too were concerned from the very beginning with the purity of the church. They sought to purify Münster by expelling from the city all who refused to be baptized, by cleansing the churches of everything that could remind people of past error, by the burning of all books except the Bible, by refusing to hire mercenaries to defend themselves because they were

---

[69]*TA Hesse*, 19; *O.O.*, 125, 399, 67; *CWMS*, 93, 94, 234, 221; *WPM*, 200-01, 294-5, 399, 443, 547; Rideman, *Confession*, 38, 155; *Hut. Ep.* I, 139; *SBR*, 156; *GZ* I, 204.

[70]*O.O.*, 399; *CWMS*, 233.

[71]Klaassen 1987B, 101.

[72]Yoder 1973, 58.

[73]*O.O.*, 304-5; *CWMS*, 750-1.

[74]*WPM*, 294-5.

[75]See the second of the Schleitheim Articles, Menno's writings on the ban; *GZ* I, 220-1, 204, 209; *WPM*, 297.

[76]*WPM*, 201.

not true believers, and by putting down all dissent with ruthless thoroughness.[77] The reasons for the purification were identical with those of other Anabaptists, but there was one more which had also motivated the Anabaptists of the Hut group earlier. That was that only the pure church could be used by God as his avenger upon the godless.

c. Chosen for vengeance

The consciousness of being God's chosen people has always been part of Jewish and Christian self understanding. This sense of chosenness has sometimes become magnified in situations of threat to the continuance of the life and integrity of the community. It was true in the Judaism of the second century B.C.E. when Antiochus IV Epiphanes attempted to turn the Jews into Greeks. That experience more than any other gave rise to apocalyptic. Early Christianity in its confrontation with the Roman Empire showed a similar response, taking over, and modifying Jewish apocalyptic to give expression to its own experience. This heightened sense of chosenness subsequently appeared within Christianity whenever dissenters within the church found their existence threatened by the majority. Examples are the Donatists, the Spiritual Franciscans, the radical Hussites, and finally, the Anabaptists. All of these experienced persecution, and that regularly had the effect of strengthening even more the sense that their remnant was the chosen people of God and that all others were unregenerate reprobates.

The sense that God had chosen for his own a small, despised, hounded group of ordinary people sustained Anabaptists in the sixteenth century and undoubtedly contributed to their survival. Let Jacob Hutter's words in a letter to Anabaptists imprisoned in the dungeon of Hohenwart Castle near Krems in Austria speak for all of Anabaptism:

> We know from the prophet Esdras and the Apostle Paul that the Lord will give eternal rest and peace to his own and no one shall offend them anymore; they shall be with God the Father and with Jesus Christ the King; they shall sit at the table in God's kingdom with Abraham, Isaac and Jacob and with all the prophets and saints of God; and they shall live with all the hosts of heaven for ever and ever.[78]

[77]van Dülmen 1974, 71-2, 89-90, 100; van Dülmen 1977, 343, but cf. van Dülmen 1974, 221-2; van Dülmen 1974, 94-6, 162-3, 227-8.

[78]Hutter 1979, 61; cf. 98.

This identification with the suffering Jesus and with his resurrection and glorification enabled them to have hope in the face of martyrdom.

But something else happened with Hut and some of his disciples and the Münsterites. For along with the conviction about being the suffering remnant, they also thought of themselves as the small army of Israel facing overwhelming odds, but winning and exterminating God's enemies because God himself had called them and led them into the battle. As in the rest of Christianity, they used the Old Testament model of the divine nation with its prophets and royal institutions to symbolize who they were. To do this with some integrity Rothmann very specifically wrote that for the time of restitution the Old Testament was primary and the New secondary.[79]

It is not an accident that in the Hut group and in Münster baptism had an expressly apocalyptic significance. Hans Hut baptized people by making the sign of the cross on their foreheads. This practice was rooted in Ezekiel 9:2-4 where we read about a man clothed in linen who was told by God to mark on the forehead all "who sigh and groan over all the abominations that are committed" in Jerusalem. This was also combined with passages in the book of Revelation 7:3-8 where an angel sealed 144,000, writing God's name on their foreheads. According to the Ezekiel passage the sign was the sign of TAU, the Hebrew letter T made in the form of a cross. The baptism was done in the name of the Father, Son, and Holy Spirit, but was identified by most of those who were later questioned about it, not as an alternative to infant baptism as in Zürich, but as the sign that one belonged to the endtime elect of God.[80] Some Anabaptists in Neustadt in Austria confessed that it was the sign of a secret covenant,[81] which was probably an allusion to being one of the elect 144,000 who had a special vocation from God. In Revelation 14:3 the 144,000 are identified as chaste, pure, and spotless, "first fruits for God and the lamb." These, according to Revelation 20:4, would reign with Christ for 1,000 years. What took place in the Netherlands beginning with Melchior Hoffman was very similar. Baptism was being sealed with the sign of TAU, by which the baptized were introduced into the mystery of faith, the true understanding of what God was then doing in the world.[82] We meet with references to the sign

[79]*SBR*, 302.

[80]See numerous cases in *QGW* II, 26,67, 79-91; *QGTÖ* I, 18-21, 24, 63, 65.

[81]*QGTÖ* I, 82.

[82]*Offenbarung*, K7a.

also in the apocalyptically charged letter of Michael Sattler to Horb,[83] in Rothmann, as one would expect,[84] and even several times in Menno Simons.[85] In the latter, however, it no longer had the earlier Melchiorite meaning.

The passage about marking people on the forehead in Ezekiel 9:4 has a horrifying sequel. For the man clothed in linen was accompanied by six executioners who were then told to slaughter without pity all who did not have the mark on their foreheads. And when the prophet protested he received the answer that God would requite upon their heads without sparing all their injustice (Ezekiel 9:5-6, 8-11). This passage, along with others, was regarded by some Anabaptists as a prediction of the future. They identified those who had received the mark, namely themselves, as the executioners.[86]

Hans Hut had inherited the view that the elect would work God's vengeance upon the ungodly from Thomas Müntzer. When the peasants had disqualified themselves as God's elect people by their failure early in 1525, Hut began the search for the elect all over again. He found them in the Anabaptists whom he first met in Augsburg in May, 1526. He was baptized and became a passionate propagandist, baptizing or signing as many as he could. These should live in obedience to Jesus, to suffer whatever would be inflicted upon them without resistance. The instructions he gave and the words of his followers suggest little Anabaptist groups very much like those elsewhere. But all who had received the sign were aware that they had a task to perform whenever God would give them the signal, and that was to eradicate all evildoers, all the unjust, all oppressors. Only when that was done could Christ's kingdom of justice and peace come. They, a small company, would be the ones to survive the great tribulation in order to carry out their mandate.[87] One Anabaptist stated in Stuttgart in 1528 that they expected the Anabaptists from Zürich to join them in their campaign of divine vengeance.[88] In several instances Anabaptists rejected the charge that they wanted to bring down the government,[89] even though in their statements the authorities were

---

[83]Yoder 1973, 61.

[84]*SBR*, 287.

[85]*O.O.*, 183, 636; *CWMS*, 59, 416.

[86]*QGW* II, 168-9.

[87]Wappler, 231, 235, 242, 244; *QGW* II, 19, 55, 148, 212; *TA Hesse*, 54.

[88]*QGW* I, 915.

[89]*QGW* II, 43, 79, 80, 86, 87.

always included among those to be exterminated. These people were clearly distinguishing uprising against government as had happened in the peasant revolt, from the divine vengeance upon all oppressors, including governments, in the End. It was the difference between revolution and what James Stayer has called "apocalyptic crusade."[90]

The story in the Netherlands followed a similar, though much more dramatic pattern. It began with Melchior Hoffman who provided the basic biblical interpretation. There were the elect marked with the sign on the forehead. There were the 144,000 special witnesses, for whom, however, Hoffman did not prescribe the role of avengers. That was, he said, not the function of God's people, but rather of constituted government.[91] But he predicted that God's exterminating wrath would fall on all the godless.[92] He protested that his frequent statements on the subject were not motivated by vengeance but that he simply stated what had been predicted.[93] And since this vengeance was part of God's intention, he, Hoffman, would not try to prevent it.[94]

In the Münster of Jan Matthijs and Jan van Leiden the final step was taken. Not only were there threats of vengeance; like the Hut people, and following similar perceptions of biblical prophecy, the Münsterites came to the conviction that they were to be God's sword of retribution. Bernhard Rothmann, the theologian and biblical scholar, became the advocate and apologist for their vision. Some say, he wrote, that God would come with his angels for retribution. He will certainly come, but before that happens, his servants will execute God's judgment upon the godless. All who did not bear the sign of TAU were marked for destruction.[95] There was a time when suffering was God's will for his people.[96] But that belonged to the second age. In the third age, which was about to begin, God would put the sword into the hands of his elect to carry out his will.[97] The time had come to advance

---

[90]Klaassen 1981A.

[91]*Weissagung*, D3a; *Romeren*, T6a, V1a.

[92]*Weissagung*, B1a, D3a; *Tuchenisse*, A7b; *Unterrichtung*, A7a.

[93]*Romeren*, Z1b; *QGT* VIII, 18.

[94]*Romeren*, V1a.

[95]*SBR*, 292, 356, 287.

[96]*SBR*, 280.

[97]*SBR*, 282, 332, 333, 347, 348, 353, 359.

from turning swords into ploughshares (Isa. 2:4) to turning ploughshares into swords (Joel 3:10).[98] God's people were ready the weapons were to hand, they were waiting only for God to give them his signal.[99] Before the signal came, the joint Catholic-Protestant armies which surrounded the city, acting on betrayal from within, burst into Münster and drowned the vision of these apocalyptic crusaders in their own blood.

That was the end of the Anabaptist flirtation with apocalyptic greatness. Expectations of the endtime, however, did not diminish for a long time. Its drumbeat can be felt in the last letters of Jacob Hutter, in the writings of Pilgram Marpeck and Menno Simons. But they had resigned themselves to living at the interface between the second and third ages, a combination of the time of suffering and the internally guiding and renewing Spirit of God. The promise of the divine kingdom, the time of justice and peace, was to be found in the struggling little churches, under constant assault from the territorial governments and churches. They still uttered imprecations of God's judgment on their oppressors and persecutors. They continued in the conviction that their little company were God's elect people. When Christ returned the great harvesting and treading of the winepress of God's wrath would elevate them into god's presence with its incredible rewards, and plunge their former oppressors into the terrible infinity of God's unconditional judgment.

[98]*SBR*, 296, 353.
[99]*SBR*, 293.

VII. Apocalyptic and History

The earlier judgment that apocalyptic among Anabaptists was limited mostly to some South German and Dutch Anabaptists is fully supported by this study.[1]   While apocalyptic was perhaps more pervasive among Swiss Anabaptists than had earlier been acknowledged, it was certainly much more restrained. Swiss Anabaptists had no Hans Hut or Melchior Hoffman. The only overt expression of apocalyptic fervour was the procession of Zollikon Anabaptists in Zürich in July, 1525. For the rest, apocalyptic sentiments appear to have been limited to apocalyptic language and imagery that was already in the public domain. It appears that the limited role of apocalyptic among Swiss Anabaptists can be accounted for, first, by the strong humanist cast of the earliest leaders. Erasmus would not even use the current antichrist language about the pope,[2] and Zwingli had virtually no interest in apocalyptic. Second, it may be that the incipient democracy and "republicanism" of Swiss canton and confederacy, in which the distance between rulers and people was not as great as elsewhere, made the ruling powers of both church and government less demonic in the eyes of the Anabaptists.[3]

The new movement begun by Martin Luther had been greeted in the German lands with great enthusiasm. Among artisans and peasants in town and village Luther's preaching about the freedom of the Christian man and his flaying of the old Church for its rapacious fleecing of the sheep of its own flock was especially welcome. The traditional pre-Reformation linking of the demands for a greater measure of both religious and economic liberty which we find, typically, in the *Twelve Articles of the Peasants*, was rejected by Luther as a perversion of the gospel. His violent response to peasant strivings alienated many. The much higher degree of both apocalyptic language as applied to current events and persons, and the assuming of God-appointed roles in the events of the End among Anabaptists and others following immediately upon the disaster of the Peasant War, is attributable at least in part to the vast disappointment of ordinary people with the Reformation. Attacks upon Martin Luther and his followers, often referred to as "the new evangelicals" or "the new papacy", were as vicious as any upon the papal Church itself. It is true that much popular literature on the subject of the Antichrist and the woes of

---

[1]Friedmann 1973, 101-15; *ME* II, 248; *ME* I, 557-9.

[2]Bainton 1969, 175-6, 218.

[3]See Brady 1985.

the Endtime had been in circulation since the beginning of the century and before. In much of that literature the papacy and the clergy as a whole had been identified with all the demonic monsters and incarnations of evil drawn from biblical apocalyptic and medieval prophecy. Still, the ferocity of the popular attack on the "evangelical" scholars points to the conviction among ordinary people that now even the preaching of the pure gospel, with which the Reformers were often credited, had been perverted by the Old Deceiver through his agent the Antichrist. This terrible betrayal of hope was seen as the last piece of evidence that the End was very near.

Many of these same dynamics were operative in the Netherlands as well, for Luther's writings were distributed there early in considerable numbers.[4] An important preparation for the effectiveness of Luther's teaching was the appearance of a number of Bible translations prior to 1530, in both Frisian and Dutch.[5] On the other hand, popular apocalyptic literature in the Dutch language was virtually nonexistent. The major bibliographies of printed books of the sixteenth century offer fewer than ten such items, in marked contrast to the hundreds available in German.[6] Most of these deal with the subjects found also in the German tracts such as *The Fifteen Signs* which were to precede the return of Christ,[7] and a collection of the prophecies of Reynhard and Methodius and other prognostications.[8] What appears to have been the most important one was published in 1523 under the sponsorship of Duke Charles of Gelderland. It was an attack upon Luther as forerunner of the Antichrist, written by a Franciscan named Henricus.[9] That apocalyptic expectation nevertheless ran so high in the Netherlands seems attributable to two factors. One was the dire economic straits of the Netherlands in the early 1530s described by Albert Mellink, a combination of inflation, warfare, food blockades, shifts in the textile industry, unemployment and migration of artisans.[10] Another was the arrival in 1530 of an unusually charismatic leader and orator, Melchior Hoffman, who with his announcement of the nearness of the End and his linking of contemporary events with that End, was able to capture the attention and fire the imagination and loyalty of enough artisans

[4]Lindsay 1911, 228-31.

[5]van der Woude 1963, 122-4.

[6]Knuttel 1890-1920 and Machiels 1979.

[7]*Tekenen.*

[8]*Tzydunge.*

[9]*Tijt Endechristus.*

[10]Mellink 1954, 1-19, 362-5.

and peasants to create an apocalyptic movement. The role of this charismatic leader should not be underestimated in the search for the causes of the apocalyptic character of Dutch Anabaptism in its first five years. No doubt Hoffman's message of the nearness of God's coming for judgment was linked to the anxiety and uncertainty caused by the social dislocation, deprivation and suffering of the people in the Netherlands in 1530. His successors Jan Matthijs and Jan van Leiden were able to offer these same people a city of refuge where divine justice was already established, and assign them a special role in God's coming judgment. Given the prevalence of apocalyptic expectation, its espousal by noted church men and women over the previous centuries, and Martin Luther's publicly attested anticipation of the early return of Christ, it would be a serious error simply to consign the apocalyptic hopes of the Radical Reformation to the bedlam of history. Apocalyptic was certainly a function of worsening social and political conditions as Norman Cohn has shown,[11] but it can also be a motor for social events, as apparently it was in sixteenth century Europe.

The common European conviction in the 1520s that the End was near produced in some quarters a short-range view of how to respond to the future. If the End is near, there is no point in making long-range plans. Long-range plans and visions emerge when apocalyptic expectation wanes as happened in the fourth and fifth centuries C. E. when the conversion of Constantine came to be seen as the beginning of the Millennium. It happened again in the seventeenth century, for example through the work of Francis Bacon.[12] But in the sixteenth century few Europeans expected a "brave new world"; rather they feared their world's final demise. The Reformation was not seen as the beginning of the "modern" period of history but as the prelude to the End of all history. Martin Luther made no plans at all at the beginning except to complete his translation of the Bible, and only reluctantly saw that something new had to replace what had been rejected. Perhaps this is an additional explanation for the ease with which the Reformation fell into the hands of the Princes. With respect to the Radical Reformation, it is entirely possible that the ecclesiologies of Anabaptism with their rigorous discipline and the constant alarmist admonitions of the leaders and martyrs for faithfulness to Christ, were understood to be short-range holding actions to preserve the church pure for the return of its Head. That would mean that the concentration on the forms of congregational life and holiness never did, in their minds, constitute an

---

[11]Cohn 1970, 14-15.

[12]See Eiseley 1973.

alternative ecclesiology for the future, but that it became such when the apocalyptic expectations were not fulfilled.

It is a brave or else foolhardy person who presumes to write intellectual history in a time when social history dominates the field. While this volume will certainly be classified as intellectual history or alas, even as theology, it needs to be said now emphatically that apocalyptic effectively removes the artificial distinction between intellectual and social history. For since its beginnings apocalyptic has been concretely historical and not at all abstract, and it is precisely at this point that it is distinguished from eschatology. Throughout the foregoing treatment this concreteness has been evident, since apocalyptic imagery was used for contemporary persons, institutions, and events. It was a description of history already happening or about to happen. The great restitution or restoration was to take place on this earth and was seen as inseparably continuous with contemporary events. Europeans had always known that God was the final mover of history, and that what was to be in the future would grow out of the present, although planned and executed by God. The Radical Reformation took that with the utmost seriousness. Its apocalyptic spokesmen fervently believed what they found in the Bible, namely, that human agents who were now active, and who with the eye of faith could recognize the signs of the times, would be deputized by God to carry out his will. In baptism they would voluntarily and deliberately become covenanters (*Bundgenossen*) and through it they would be equipped with the Spirit of power and wisdom in order to be equal to the task. The commitment to the "apocalyptic crusade" was in no essential different from moderns joining the cause of a revolution that has a vision of justice and peace for the future.

Those in South Germany and the Netherlands who were committed to the apocalyptic vision, resembled some modern revolutionaries in that they believed that the world would first have to be cleansed of all evil, of all infection from the past, before God's new earth and heaven could become reality. It was this fierce dedication to purity that led to the conviction that all who did not bear the mark of the apocalyptic covenant would have to be exterminated. They extended forward into the preparation for the Holy City its purity, and, in order to achieve that purity, they were prepared to exterminate all "the cowardly, the faithless, the polluted, . . .murderers, fornicators, sorcerers, idolaters, and all liars [whose] lot shall be in the lake that burns with fire and brimstone. . . . Nothing unclean shall enter it, nor anyone who practices abomination or falsehood, but only those whose names are written in the Lamb's book of life." (RSV Rev. 21:8, 27). And they presumed to know whose names were in the Lamb's book and whose not. They historicized the myth, and in so doing struck cold fear into the hearts of their contemporaries. It was this feature of sixteenth century apocalyptic that produced the high alarm that is so evident in the polemics against the Münster Anabaptists. It was this that quickly sealed their fate.

The sixteenth century was impatient with visionaries as indeed is any age, since visionaries, implicitly or explicitly, challenge the status quo. The existing powers in church and state struck back with a vengeance at any vision of society which proposed to displace and dispossess the powerholders. The apocalyptic vision was not abstract theology or religion. It was a very present and serious threat because it put in question all existing religious, societal, and political arrangements *sub specie aeternitatis.*

It must by now be evident that the author takes a didactic view of history. It is instructive to look closely at this episode of western history even though we encounter much there that repels us and that we reject with horror. It is also evident that apocalyptic is not passe but of contemporary relevance. The Melchior Hoffmans and the Hans Huts are still with us although under new names and management. We can see them by television virtually every day. They tell us not to worry about the troubles in the world, because God will provide a refuge for all his born-again people by removing them from the world as it begins to burn. Not only that, but they have had, and may have again, places close to the formation of national policy.[13] Some of them seem quite ready to hold the flame to the kindling and try to force God's hand like Jan Matthijs and Jan van Leiden. All these, the Huts, the Hoffmans, the Jan Matthijs', and the Jan van Leidens were true believers. They suffered from self-righteousness born of burning resentments and from the illusions of false hopes of all revolutionaries past and present. Meanwhile the corpses pile up. They are warnings never to confuse "the kingdoms of this world" with "the kingdom of our Lord and of his Christ" (RSV Rev. 11:15). There is and can be no perfection in any social order devised by human beings. Particularly pernicious and dangerous is the conceit that there can ever be human beings so perfect that they can claim divine omniscience and so pass judgment on everyone else. Perhaps this story will remind us again of these dangers.

[13]See Bater 1988 and Halsell 1988.

References to Footnotes

Anderson 1932
Anderson, A. R. *Alexander's Gate, Gog and Magog, and the Inclosed Nations,*
Cambridge, Mass.: Harvard University Press, 1932.

Archer 1958
Archer, G. L. *Jerome's Commentary on Daniel,* Grand Rapids: Baker Book
House, 1958

Aufdeckung
Hillerbrand, H. J. "An Early Anabaptist Treatise on the Christian and the
State"' *MQR* 32 (1958), 28-47.

Bainton 1936
Bainton, R. H. "Changing Ideas and Ideals in the Sixteenth Century", *Journal
of Modern History* 8 (1936), 417-43.

Bainton 1969
Bainton, R. H. *Erasmus of Rotterdam,* New York: Scribners, 1969.

Bapstesel
[P. Melanchthon & M. Luther], *Deuttung der zwo grewlichen Figuren
Bapstesels zu .Rom vnd Munchkalbs zv freyberg jn Meissen. Philippus
Melanchthon Doct. Martinus luther. Wittemberg, M. D. xxiij.*

Bater 1988
Bater, R. "Arming for Armageddon"' *Peace Magazine* 3 (Dec. 1987- Jan.
1988), 8-9.

Blanke 1952
Blanke, F. "Die Propheten von Zollikon (1525)", *Mennonitische
Geschichtsblätter* 9 (1952), 2-10.

Blanke 1961
Blanke F. *Brothers in Christ,* Scottdale: Herald Press, 1961.

Bossert 1914
Bossert G. "Augustin Bader von Augsburg, der Prophet und König, und seine Genossen nach den Prozessakten von 1530", *Archiv für Reformationsgeschichte* 11 (1914), 19-64, 103-33, 176-99.

Brady 1985
Brady, T. A. *Turning Swiss: Cities and Empire 1450-1550*, Cambridge: Cambridge University Press, 1985.

Buchanan 1956
Buchanan, H. "Luther and the Turks," *ARG* 47 (1956), 145-60.

Burger 1986
Burger, E. K. ed. *Joachim of Fiore: Enchiridion super Apocalypsim*, Toronto: Pontifical Institute of Medieval Studies, 1986.

Classen 1928
Classen, Peter. "Eschatologische Ideen und Armutsbewegungen im 11. und 12. Jahrhundert", *Poverta e ricchezza nella spiritualita dei secoli XI e XII* 8 (1969), 129-62.

Clemen 1928
Clemen, Otto. "Schriften und Lebensausgang des Eisenacher Franziskaners Johann Hiltens", *Zeitschrift für Kirchengeschichte* 47 (1928), 402-12.

Cohn
Cohn, N. *The Pursuit of the Millennium: Revolutionary Millenarians and Mystical Anarchists of the Middle Ages*, 3rd ed. New York: Oxford University Press, 1970.

Concordia
Joachim of Fiore, *Concordia Novi ac Veteris Testamenti*, Venice, 1519

CS
Corpus Schwenckfeldianorum, ed. C. D. Hartranft et al 19 vols., Norristown and Pennsburg: The Board of Publication of the Schwenkfelder Church, 1907-1961.

Cornelius 1853
Cornelius C. A. hrg. *Berichte der Augenzeugen über das münsterische Wiedertäuferreich*, Münster: Asschendorff, 1983 reprint of 1853 edition.

Chronik
Die älteste Chronik der hutterischen Brüder, bearb. A. J. F. Zieglschmid, Carl Schurz Memorial Foundation, 1943.

CWMS
The Complete Writings of Menno Simons, ed. J. C. Wenger, Scottdale: Herald Press, 1956.

DAN I
Documenta Anabaptistica Neerlandica. Eerste Deel: Friesland en Groningen 1530-1550, ed. A. F. Mellink, Leiden: Brill, 1975.

Dawson 1958
Dawson, Christopher. *Religion and the Rise of Western Culture*, New York: Doubleday, 1958.

Deppermann 1979
Deppermann, Klaus. *Melchior Hoffman: Soziale Unruhen und apokalyptische Visionen im Zeitalter der Reformation*, Göttingen: Vandenhoeck und Ruprecht, 1979.

DS
Hans Denck: Schriften, 2. Teil. Religiöse Schriften, hrg. Walter Fellmann, Gütersloh: Bertelsmann, 1956.

Dethlefs 1983
Dethlefs, Gerd. "Das Wiedertäuferreich in Münster 1534/35", *Die Wiedertäufer in Münster*, Münster: Stadtmuseum Münster, 1983, 19-36.

Dillenberger 1961
Dillenberger, J. ed. *Martin Luther: Selections from His Writings*, New York: Doubleday, 1961.

Eiseley 1973
Eiseley, Loren. *The Man Who Saw Through Time*, New York: Scribners, 1973.

Emmerson
Emmerson, R. K. *Antichrist in the Middle Ages*, Manchester: Manchester University Press, 1981.

Endtkrist 1505
Dys büchlein sagt von des Endtkrists leben vnnd regierung, etc., [Woodcuts],
M. Maler: Erffordt, 1505.

Expositio
Joachim of Fiore, *Expositio in Apocalypsim*, Venice, 1527.

Fast 1962
Fast, H. *Der Linke Flügel der Reformation*, Bremen: Carl Schünemann Verlag,
1962

Franck, *Chronica*
Chronika, Zeitbuch vnnd Geschichtsbibell . . ., Ulm, 1536.

Fremantle 1956
Fremantle, A. ed. *The Papal Encyclicals in Their Historical Context*, New
York: New American Library, 1956.

Friedman 1978
Friedman, J. *Michael Servetus: A Case Study in Total Heresy*, Geneve:
Librairie Droz S. A., 1978.

Friedmann 1973
Friedmann, R. *The Theology of Anabaptism*, Scottdale: Herald Press, 1973.

Friesen & Klaassen
Sixteenth Century Anabaptism: Defences, Confessions, Refutations, transl. F.
Friesen, ed. W. Klaassen, Conrad Grebel College, 1982.

GZ I
Glaubenszeugnisse oberdeutscher Taufgesinnter, ed. L. Müller, New York:
Johnson Reprint Corp., 1971.

GZ II
Glaubenszeugnisse oberdeutscher Taufgesinnter II, ed. R. Friedmann,
Gütersloher Verlagshaus Gerd Mohn, 1967.

Goertz 1982
Goertz, H.-J. *Profiles of Radical Reformers*, Scottdale: Herald Press, 1982.

Goertz 1987
Goertz, H.-J. *Pfaffenhass und Gross Geschrei: Die Reformatorischen Bewegungen in Deutschland 1517-1529*, München: Beck, 1987.

Goertz 1989
Goertz, H.-J. *Thomas Müntzer: Mystiker, Apokalyptiker, Revolutionär*, München: Beck, 1989.

Goeters 1957
Goeters, J. F. G. *Ludwig Hätzer (ca. 1500-1529) Spiritualist und Antitrinitarier. Eine Randfigur der frühen Täuferbewegung*, Gütersloh: C. Bertelsmann Verlag, 1957.

Grosheide I
Grosheide, G. "Verhooren en Vonnissen der Wederdopers, Betrokken bij de Aanslagen op Amsterdam in 1534 en 1535", *Bijdragen en Mededeelingen van het Historisch Genootschap*, 41 (1920), 1-197.

Halsell 1988
Halsell, Grace. "Courting Armageddon: The Politics of Christian Zionism", *The Other Side*, January/February, 1988, 28-31.

Harder
Harder, L. ed. *The Sources of Swiss Anabaptism*, Scottdale: Herald Press, 1985.

Hartfelder 1889
Hartfelder, Karl. "Der Aberglaube Ph. Melanchthons", *Historisches Taschenbuch* 6. Folge, 8. Jg., 1889, 237ff.

Headley 1963
Headley, J. M. *Luther's View of Church History*, New Haven: Yale University Press, 1963.

Hill 1971
Hill, Christopher. *Antichrist in Seventeenth-Century England*, London: Oxford University Press, 1971.

Hillerbrand 1959
Hillerbrand, H. J. "Ein Täuferbekenntnis aus dem 16. Jahrhundert", *ARG* 50 (1959), 40-50.

Hillerbrand 1967
Hillerbrand, H. J. *A Fellowship of Discontent*, New York: Harper & Row, 1967.

Hillerbrand 1971
Hillerbrand, H. J. "Anabaptism and History", *MQR* 45 (1971), 107-22.

Hillerdal 1954
Hillerdal, G. "Prophetische Züge in Luthers Geschichtsdeutung", *Studia Theologica* 7 (1954), 105-24.

Holl 1923
Holl, Karl. "Luther und die Schwärmer", *Gesammelte Aufsätze zur Kirchengeschichte I*, Tübingen, 1923.

Hoffman, Melchior, Works

Amsdorf
"Das Niclas Amsdorff der Magdeburger Pastor ein lugenhaftiger falscher nasen geist sey, offentlich bewiesen durch Melchior Hoffman 1528", *Schriften des Vereins für Schleswig-Holsteinische Kirchengeschichte*, Sonderheft 4, 1926.

Cantica Canticorum
Dat Boeck Cantica Canticorum: edder dat hoge leedt Salomonis . . ., Kyll, M. D. XXIX.

Daniel XII
Das XII Capitel des propheten Danielis aussgelegt . . ., Stockholm: Königliche Druckerei, 1526.

Das ware trostliche...Euangelion
Horst, I. B. & D. Visser, "Een Tractaat van Melchior Hoffman uit 1531", *Doopsgezinde Bijdragen* 4 (1978), 66-81.

Derpten
Der Christlichen gemeyn zu Derpten . . ., Wittenberg: Lotter, 1525.

Dialogus
Dialogus und grundtliche berichtung gehaltener disputation . . ., 1529, [Strassburg].

Gesicht
Prophetische Gesicht vnd Offenbarung/der götlichen wurckung zu diser letsten zeit . . ., M. D. XXX

Judas
Die Epistel des Apostell Sanct Judas . . ., Hagenau: Kobian, 1534

Lifland
An de gelovighen vorsamblung inn Liflandt ein korte formaninghe . . ., 1526, publ. by A. Buchholtz 1856.

Majestät
Van der hochprachtlichen eynigen magestadt gottes . . ., Deventer: Paffraet, 1532. A modern transcription in S. Voolstra, *Het Woord is Vlees Geworden*, Kampen: Uitgeversmaatschappij J. H. Kok, 1982, 229-245.

Offenbarung
Ausslegung der heimlichen Offenbarung Joannis . . ., Strassburg: Beck, 1530.

Prophecey
Prophecey oder weissagung vss warer heiliger götlicher schrifft ..., 1530

Romeren
Die eedele hoghe ende troostlike sendebrief/den die heylige Apostel Paulus to den Romeren gescreuen heeft . . ., 1533.

Sendbrieff
Eyn sendbrieff an alle gottsförchtigen . . ., Hagenau: Kobian, 1533.

Tuchenisse
Een waraftyghe tuchenisse vnde gruntlyke verclarynge . . ., Deventer: Paffraet, 1532.

Unterrichtung
Ein rechte warhafftige hohe vnd göttliche grundliche vnnderichtung von der reiner forchte gottes . . ., 1533.

Weyssagung
Weyssagung ausz Heiliger Gotlicher geschrifft . . ., 1530.

Zeucknus
*Das freudenreiche zeuchnus vam worren friderichen ewigen evangelion .
. .,* in F. O. zur Linden, *Melchior Hofmann,* Haarlem, 1885, 429-432.

Hubmaier
Balthasar Hubmaier: Schriften, ed. G. Westin & T. Bergsten, Gütersloher
Verlagshaus Gerd Mohn, 1962.

Hut. Ep. I,
Hut. Ep. II
Die Hutterischen Epistel 1525 bis 1767, vols I & II publ. by Die Hutterischen
Brüder in Amerika, Elie, Man.: James Valley Book Centre, 1986.

Hutter 1979
Brotherly Faithfulness: Epistles from a Time of Persecution, Rifton, N. Y.:
Plough Publishing House, 1979.

Jonas
Jonas, Justus. *Das sibende Capitel Danielis, von/des Türcken Gottes/ lestrung
vnd schreck/licher morederey,/mit vnter/richt/* . . ., Wittemberg, 1530.

Klaassen 1978
Klaassen, Walter. *Michael Gaismair: Revolutionary and Reformer,* Leiden:
Brill, 1978.

Klaassen 1978A
Klaassen, W. "Church Discipline and the Spirit in Pilgram Marpeck", *De Geest
in het Geding,* ed. I. B. Horst et al, Alphen an den Rijn: Tjeenk Willink, 1978,
169-80.

Klaassen 1981
Klaassen, W. ed. *Anabaptism in Outline: Selected Primary Sources,* Scottdale:
Herald Press, 1981.

Klaassen 1981A
Klaassen, W. "Doperdom als revolutie: een voorbeeld van 'confessionalisme'
in de doopsgezinde geschiedschrijvinng", *DB* 7, (1981), 109-15.

Klaassen 1986
Klaassen, W. "The Abomination of Desolation: Schwenckfeld's Christological Apocalyptic", *Schwenckfeld and Early Schwenkfeldianism*, ed. Peter C. Erb, Pennsburg: Schwenkfeklder Library, 1986.

Klaassen 1986A
Klaassen, W. "Eschatological Themes in Early Dutch Anabaptism", *The Dutch Dissenters*, ed. I. B. Horst, Leiden: Brill, 1986.

Klaassen 1987
Klaassen, W. "Investigation into the Authorship and the Historical Background of the Anabaptist Tract 'Aufdeckung der Babylonischen Hurn . . .'", *MQR* 61 (1987), 251-61.

Klaassen 1987A
Klaassen, W. "Die Taufe im Schweizer Täufertum", *MGB* 46 (1989), 75-89.

Klaassen 1987B
Klaassen, W. "The 'Schleitheim Articles' and the 'New Transformation of Christian Living': Two Responses to the Reformation", *Historical Reflections* 14 (1987), 95-112.

Klaassen 1987C
Klaassen, W. "'Of Divine and Human Justice'" unpubl. lecture, J. J. Thiessen Lectures, Canadian Mennonite Bible College, Oct. 1987.

Klassen 1968
Klassen, William. *Covenant and Community*, Grand Rapids: Eerdman's, 1968.

Kmosko 1931
Kmosko, M. "Das Rätsel des Pseudomethodius", *Byzantion* 6 (1931)

Knappert 1924
Knappert, L. "De Nederlandsche 'Prognosticon de antichristo' 1524 teruggevonden," *Nederlandsch Archief voor Kerkgeschiedenis* XVII (1924).

Knuttel
Knuttel, W. P. C. *Catalogus van de Pamflettenverzameling*, berustende in de *Koninklijke Bibliotheek*, s'Gravenhage : Algemeene Landsdrukkerij, 1889-1920.

Koch 1965
Koch, J. "Die Grundlagen der Geschichtsphilosophie Ottos von Freising," *Geschichtsdenken und Geschichtsbild im Mittelalter* hrg. W. Lammers, Darmstadt: Wissenschaftliche Buchgesellschaft, 1965.

Konrad 1964
Konrad, R. *De Ortu et de tempore Antichristi. Antichristvorstellung und Geschichtsbild des Abtes Adso von Montier-en-Der*, Kallmünz, 1964, 54-70.

Köstlin 1878
Köstlin, J. "Ein Beitrag zur Eschatologie der Reformatoren," *Theologische Studien und Kritiken* 51 (1878), 125-35.

Kühler 1961
Kühler, W. J. *Geschiedenis der Nederlandsche Doopsgezinden in de Zestiende Eeuw*, Haarlem: Tjeenk Willink, 1961.

Kurze 1956
Kurze, D. "Johannes Lichtenberger: Leben und Werk eines spätmittelalterlichen Propheten und Astrologen," *Archiv für Kulturgeschichte* 38 (1956), 328-43.

Lambert 1977
Lambert, M. D. *Medieval Heresy: Popular Movements from Bogomil to Hus*, London: Edward Arnold, 1977.

Lammers 1974
Lammers, Walther hrg. *Ottonis episcopi Frisingensis: Chronica sive historia de duabus civitatibus - Otto Bischof von Freising: Chronik oder die Geschichte der zwei Staaten*, Darmstadt: Wissenschaftliche Buchgesellschaft, 1974.

Lichtenberger
[Lichtenberger, Johannes], *Die Weissagungen Johannis Lichtenbergers deudsch/zugericht mit vleys Sampt einer nutzlichen vorrede vnd vnntericht D. Martini Luthers/ Wie man die selbige vnd der gleichen weissagungen vernemen sol*, Wittemberg, M.D.xxvij.

Lilje 1932
Lilje, Hanns. *Luthers Geschichtsanschauung*, Berlin, 1932.

Linden 1885
Linden, Otto zur. *Melchior Hofmann, ein Prophet der Wiedertäufer*, Haarlem: de Erven F. Bohn, 1885.

Lindsay 1911
Lindsay, T. M. *A History of the Reformation II*, New York: Scribners, 1911.

Lindsey 1970
Lindsey, Hal. *The Late Great Planet Earth*, Grand Rapids: Zondervan, 1970.

Lindsey 1984
Lindsey, Hal. *There's a New World Coming*, Eugene, Ore.: Harvest House, 1984.

List 1973
List, G. *Chiliastische Utopie*, München: Fink Verlag, 1973

Littell 1958
Littell, F. H. *The Anabaptist View of the Church*, 2d. ed. Boston: Star King Press, 1958.

Littell 1971
Littell, F. H. "In Response to Hans Hillerbrand," *MQR* 45 (1971), 377-80.

Lockwood 1969
Lockwood, W. B. "Vernacular Scriptures in Germany and in the Low Countries before 1500," *The Cambridge History of the Bible: The West from the Fathers to the Reformation*, ed. G. W. Lampe, Cambridge: Cambridge University Press, 1969, 415-36.

Luth Chron
Chronica des Ehrnwirdigen Herrn D. Mart. Luth. Deudsch, Witteberg: Hans Lufft, 1559. Translated and introduced by J. Aurifaber. A translation of the Latin *Supputatio annorum mundi*, 1541.

Machiels 1979
Catalogus van de boeken gedruckt voor 1600 aanwezig op de Central Bibliotheek van de Rijksuniversiteit Gent, ed. J. Machiels, 2 vols., Gent: Centrale Bibliotheek, 1979.

McGinn 1975
McGinn, B. "Apocalypticism in the Middle Ages: an Historiographical Sketch," *Medieval Studies* 37 (1975), 252-86.

McGinn 1978
McGinn, B. "Angel Pope and Papal Antichrist," *Church History*, 47 (1978), 155-73.

McGinn 1979
McGinn, B. *Visions of the End: Apocalyptic Traditions in the Middle Ages*, New York: Columbia University Press, 1979.

McGinn 1979A
McGinn, B. *Apocalyptic Spirituality*, New York: Paulist Press, 1979.

McGinn 1985
McGinn, B. *The Calabrian Abbott: Joachim of Fiore in the History of Western Thought*, New York: Macmillan, 1985.

ME
The Mennonite Encyclopedia, ed. H. S. Bender et al, 4 vols., Scottdale: Mennonite Publishing House, 1955-1959.

Meihuizen 1954
Meihuizen, H. W. "De verwachting van de wederkomende Christus en het rijk Gods bij de oude Doopsgezinden," *Stemmen uit de Doopsgezinde Broederschap*, III (1954), 42-50.

Meihuizen 1970
Meihuizen, H. W. "The Concept of Restitution in the Anabaptism of Northwestern Europe," *MQR* 44 (1970), 141-58.

Mellink 1954
Mellink, A. *De Wederdopers in de noordelijke Nederlanden 1531-1544*, Groningen: J. B. Wolters, 1954.

Menke-Glückert 1912
Menke-Glückert, Emil. *Die Geschichtsschreibung der Reformation und Gegenreformation*, Leipzig, 1912.

Meuthen 1959
Meuthen, E. *Kirche und Heilsgeschichte bei Gerhoh von Reichersberg,* Leiden-Köln, 1959.

Meyer 1874
Meyer, C. "Die Anfänge des Wiedertäuferthums in Augsburg," *Zeitschrift des historischen Vereins für Schwaben und Neuburg,* I, 1874, 207-53.

Moore 1975
Moore, R. I. *The Birth of Popular Heresy,* London: Edward Arnold, 1975.

Offenbarungen
Namhaffter offennbarungen zwo. Aine sagt der Allt Joachim. Die Annder die heylig fraw Hilldegradis, so inen von gott geoffenbart ist worden, etc. [1520].

O.O.
Opera Omnia Theologica of alle de Godtgeleerde Wercken van Menno Symons, ed. H. J. Herrison, Amsterdam: van Veen, 1681.

Osiander, Hildegard
Sant Hildegardten weissagung über die papisten . . .eyn vorred durch A. Osiander, 1527.

Ozment 1973
Ozment, S. E. *Mysticism and Dissent: Religious Ideology and Social Protest in the Sixteenth Century,* New Haven: Yale University Press, 1973.

Packull 1977
Packull. W. O. *The Early South German-Austrian Anabaptist Movement 1525-1531,* Scottdale: Herald Press, 1977.

Packull 1986
Packull, W. O. "A Reinterpretation of Melchior Hoffman's 'Exposition' Against the Background of the Spiritualist Franciscan Eschatology with Special Reference to Peter John Olivi," *The Dutch Dissenters,* ed. I. B. Horst, Leiden: Brill, 1986.

Packull 1986A
Packull, W. O. "The Schwenkfeldian Commentary on the Apocalypse," *Schwenckfeld and Early Schwenkfeldianism,* ed. Peter C. Erb, Pennsburg : Schwenkfelder Library, 1986, 47-86.

Pater 1984
Pater, C. A. *Karlstadt as the Father of the Baptist Movements: The Emergence of Lay Protestantism*, Toronto: University of Toronto Press, 1984.

Peters 1972
Ulrich Zwingli (1484-1531) Selected Works, ed. S. M. Jackson, introd. E. Peters, Philadelphia: University of Pennsylvania Press, 1972.

Peukert 1966
Peukert, W.-E. *Die Grosse Wende: Das apokalyptische Saeculum und Luther*, 2 Bde. Darmstadt: Wissenschaftliche Buchgesellschaft, 1966.

Pflanz 1939
Pflanz, H.-H. *Geschichte und Eschatologie bei Martin Luther*, Stuttgart, 1939.

Philips
Dietrich Philip. Enchiridion or Hand Book, Aylmer, Ont.: Pathway, 1978.

Preuss 1906
Preuss, Hans. *Die Vorstellungen vom Antichrist im späteren Mittelalter bei Luther und in der konfessionellen Polemik*, Leipzig, 1906.

Preuss 1933
Preuss, H. *Luther: Der Prophet*, Gütersloh, 1933.

Psalterium
Joachim of Fiore, *Psalterium decem cordarum*, Venice, 1527. Reprinted Frankfurt a.M.: Minerva, 1965.

Purvey
Purvey, John. *Remonstrance against Romish Corruptions in the Church, addressed to the people and Parliament in 1395, ... Now for the first time published*. Ed. J. Forstall, London, 1851.

QGT IV
Quellen zur Geschichte der Täufer IV. Bd. Baden und Pfalz, hrg. M. Krebs, Gütersloh: Bertelsmann, 1951.

QGT V
Quellen zur Geschichte der Täufer V. Bd. Bayern II. Abteilung, hrg. K. Schornbaum, Gütersloh: Bertelsmann, 1951.

QGT VII
*Quellen zur Geschichte der Täufer VII. Bd. Elsass I. Teil Stadt Strassburg
1522-1532*, hrg. M. Krebs und G. Rott, Gütersloher Verlagshaus Gerd Mohn,
1959.

QGT VIII
*Quellen zur Geschichte der Täufer VIII. Bd. Elsass II. Teil Stadt Strassburg
1533-1535*, hrg. M. Krebs und G. Rott, Gütersloher Verlagshaus Gerd Mohn,
1960.

QGTÖ I
Quellen zur Geschichte der Täufer XI. Bd. Österreich I. Teil, hrg. G.
Mecenseffy, Gütersloher Verlagshaus Gerd Mohn, 1964.

QGTÖ II
Quellen zur Geschichte der Täufer Österreich II. Teil, hrg. G. Mecenseffy,
Gütersloher Verlagshaus Gerd Mohn, 1972.

QGTÖ III
Quellen zur Geschichte der Täufer Österreich III. Teil, hrg. G. Mecenseffy mit
M. Schmelzer, Gütersloher Verlagshaus Gerd Mohn, 1983.

QGTS I
Quellen zur Geschichte der Täufer in der Schweiz I. Bd. Zürich, hrg. L. von
Muralt und W. Schmid, Zürich: S. Hirzel Verlag, 1952.

QGTS II
Quellen zur Geschichte der Täufer in der Schweiz II. Bd. Ostschweiz, hrg. H.
Fast, Zürich: Theologischer Verlag, 1973.

QGTS IV
Quellen zur Geschichte der Täufer in der Schweiz IV. Bd. hrg. M. Haas,
Zürich: Theologischer Verlag, 1974.

QGW I
Quellen zur Geschichte der Wiedertäufer I. Bd. Herzogtum Württemberg, hrg.
G. Bossert, Leipzig: M. Heinsius Nachfolger, 1930.

QGW II
Quellen zur Geschichte der Wiedertäufer II. Bd. Markgraftum Brandenburg Bayern I. Abteilung, hrg. K. Schornbaum, Leipzig: M. Heinsius Nachfolger, 1934.

Rauh 1973
Rauh, Horst D. *Das Bild des Antichrist im Mittelalter: Vom Tyconius zum deutschen Symbolismus*, Münster: Aschendorff, 1973.

Reeves 1969
Reeves, M. *The Influence of Prophecy in the Later Middle Ages*, Oxford: Oxford University Press, 1969.

Reeves 1976
Reeves, M. *Joachim of Fiore and the Prophetic Future*, London: SPCK, 1976.

Reeves and Hirsch-Reich 1972
Reeves, M. and B. Hirsch-Reich, *The Figurae of Joachim of Fiore*, Oxford: Clarendon Press, 1972.

Rideman, *Confession*
Account of our Religion, Doctrine and Faith, Given by Peter Rideman ..., London: Hodder and Stoughton, 1950.

Röhrich 1860
Röhrich, T. W. "Zur Geschichte der Strassburgischen Wiedertäufer 1527-1543," *Zeitschrift für die historische Theologie* 30 Heft 1 (1860).

Rohr 1898
Rohr, J. "Die Prophetie im letzten Jahrhundert vor der Reformation als Geschichtsquelle und Geschichtsfaktor," *Historisches Jahrbuch*, 19 (1998), 29-56, 447-66.

Rosenberg 1955
Rosenberg, A. *Joachim von Fiore: Das Reich des Heiligen Geistes*, München/Planneg: Otto Wilhelm Barth-Verlag, 1955.

Rupp 1969
Rupp. G. *Patterns of Reformation*, London: Epworth, 1969.

Russell 1971
Russell, J. B. *Religious Dissent in the Middle Ages,* New York: Wiley, 1971.

Russell 1983
Russell, Paul. "'Your sons and your daughters shall prophesy ...' Common People and the Future of the Reformation in the Pamphlet Literature of Southwestern Germany to 1525," *ARG* 76 (1983), 122-40.

Russell 1985
Russell, P. *Lay Theology in the Reformation: Popular Pamphleteers in Southwest Germany 1521-1525,* Cambridge: Cambridge University Press, 1985

Sackur 1898
Sackur, E. *Sibyllinische Texte und Forschungen,* Halle a.s., 1898.

Sanchez 1972
Sanchez, Jose. *Anticlericalism: A Brief History,* Notre Dame: University of Notre Dame Press, 1972.

SB-7
Eeymundus Offenbarung. Ist gefunden worden in aynem alten Buoch/Vor vil Jaren geschriben. Die Propheteyen vnnd Weyssagungen ...durch Cirillum/ Joachim/ Brigitten/ Franciscum/ Reinhart/ vnnd Methodium etc. beschriben. M.D.XXXII

Scivias 1986
Hildegard of Bingen's Scivias, ed. A Führkötter and M. Fox, Sante Fe, N.M.: Bear & Co., 1986.

SBR
Stupperich, R. hrg. *Die Schriften Bernhard Rothmanns,* Münster: Aschendorffsche Verlagsbuchhandlung, 1970.

Schade 1854
Schade, O. *Geistliche Gedichte des XIV. und XV. Jahrhunderts vom Niederrhein,* Hannover, 1854.

Scherer 1885
Scherer, W. hrg. *Passional Christi und Antichristi: Lucas Cranachs Holzschnitte mit dem Texte von Melanchthon,* Berlin: Grot'sche Verlagsbuchhandlung, 1885.

Schmid 1971
Schmid, H.-D. "Das Hutsche Täufertum," *Historisches Jahrbuch* 91 (1971), 327-44.

Schmidt 1955
Schmidt, R. "Die Welt Zeitalter als Gliederungsprinzip der Geschichte," *Zeitschrift für Kirchengeschichte* 67 (1955/1956), 288-318.

Scribner 1981
Scribner, R. W. *For the Sake of Simple Folk. Popular Propaganda for the German Reformation*, Cambridge: Cambridge University Press, 1981.

Seibt 1982
Seibt, F. "Johannes Hergot", *Profiles of Radical Reformers*, ed. H.-J Goertz, Scottdale: Herald Press, 1982.

Sendbrief
Zwen wunder seltzam sendbrieff zweyer Widertauffer/ an ire Rotten gen Augspurg gesandt. . . . Augspurg: A. Weyssenhorn, 1528.

Shumaker 1972
Shumaker, W. *The Occult Sciences in the Renaissance*, Berkeley: University of California Press, 1972.

Sigismundi
Reformatio Sigismundi (Augsburg: Lukas Zeissenmair, 1497). Neudruck Leipzig: Zentralantiquariat der DDR, 1979.

Spörl 1965
Spörl, J. "Die 'Civitas Dei' im Geschichtsdenken Ottos von Freising," *Geschichtsdenken und Geschichtsbild im Mittelalter*, hrg. W. Lammers, Darmstadt: Wissenschaftliche Buchgesellschaft, 1965.

Staehelin 1951
Staehelin, E. *Die Verkündigung des Reiches Gottes in der Kirche Jesu Christi*, 3 vols. Basel: Verlag Friedrich Reinhardt, 1951.

Steinmetz 1977
Hans Hergot und die Flugschrift 'Von der Newen Wandlung Eynes Christlichen Lebens,' Faksimilewiedergabe mit Umschrift, hrg. M. Steinmetz, Leipzig: VEB Fachbuchverlag, 1977

Strauss 1971
Strauss, G. ed. *Manifestations of Discontent on the Eve of the Reformation*, Bloomington: University of Indiana Press, 1971.

Struve 1978
Struve, T. "Reform oder Revolution? ... Reformatio Sigismundi ...," *Zeitschrift für die Geschichte des Oberrheins* 126 (1978), 73-129.

Stupperich 1983
Stupperich, R. "Das münsterische Täufertum, sein Wesen und seine Verwirklichung," *Die Wiedertäufer in Münster*, Münster: Stadtmuseum Münster, 1983, 37-54.

Swartley 1984
Swartley, W. ed. *Essays in Biblical Interpretation: Anabaptist-Mennonite Perspectives*, Elkhart: Institute of Mennonite Studies, 1984.

TA Hesse
Urkundliche Quellen zur hessischen Reformationsgeschichte IV. Bd. Wiedertäuferakten, hrg. G. Franz, Marburg:Elwert, 1951.

Tappert 1967
Tappert, T. G. ed. *Selected Writings of Martin Luther 1520-1523*, Philadelphia: Fortress Press, 1967.

Tekenen
Vijfthien vreeslijke Tekenen, die voerghan sullen dat stranghe oordeel Iehsu Chrysti [Antwerpen: Jan van Doesborch c. 1505].

Theodoricus 1530
Theodoricus, Croata. *Ain practica oder weissagung eins bruoders/ Barfuosser ordenns/ mit namen Dieterich/ beschehen zuo Zeng in Granaten/ ... ym 1420. Jar ... [Augsburg? 1530?]*.

Tijt
Van der verweerlicken aenstande Tijt Endechristes op kosten van Hartog Karel van Gelder, [Deventer: Albert Paffraet, 1523].

TMSB
Thomas Müntzer: Schriften und Briefe, hrg. G. Franz, Gütersloher Verlagshaus Gerd Mohn, 1968

Torrance 1953
Torrance, T. F. "The Eschatology of the Reformation," *Scottish Journal of Theology,* Occasional Papers No. 2, 1953, 36-63.

Tzydunge
New erbarmliche tzydunge van der groisser schlacht, [1526].

van der Woude 1963
van der Woude, S. "Continental versions to c.1600: Dutch," *The Cambridge History of the Bible: The West from the Reformation to the Present Day,* ed. S. L. Greenslade, Cambridge: Cambridge Ubniversity Press, 1963.

van Dülmen 1974
van Dülmen, R. hrg. *Das Täuferreich zu Münster 1534-1535: Dokumente,* München: DTV, 1974.

van Dülmen 1977
van Dülmen, R. *Reformation als Revolution: Soziale Bewegung und religiöser Radikalismus in der deutschen Reformation,* München: DTV, 1977.

Verhelst, D. ed. *Adso Dervensis: De Ortu et Tempore Antichristi,* Turnhout: Brepols, 1976.

Verheus 1971
Verheus, S. L. *Zeugnis und Gericht: Kirchliche Betrachtungen bei Sebastian Franck und Matthias Flacius,* Nieuwkop: de Graaf, 1971.

Vogler 1988
Vogler, G. "The Anabaptist Kingdom of Munster in the Tension Between Anabaptism and Imperial Policy," *Radical Tendencies in the Reformation,* ed. H. J. Hillerbrand, Kirksville, MO.: Sixteenth Century Journal Publishers, 1988, 99-116.

Wappler
Wappler, P. *Die Täuferbewegung in Thüringen von 1526-1584,* Jena: G. Fischer, 1913.

Wappler 1966
Wappler, P. *Thomas Müntzer in Zwickau und die 'Zwickauer Propheten',* Gütersloher Verlagshaus Gerd Mohn, 1966.

Warburg 1919
Warburg, Aby, "Heidnisch-antike Weissagungen in Wort und Bild zu Luthers Zeiten," *Sitzungsberichte der Akademie der Wissenschaften Heidelberg phil-hist. Kl., 1919: 26, Heidelberg, 1919.*

Adventspostille
D. Martin Luthers Werke. Weimar, 10/1/2, 93-120.

WA DB
D. Martin Luthers Werke. Deutsche Bibel, Weimar, 1906-1961.

Williams 1957
Williams, G. H. *Spiritual and Anabaptist Writers,* Philadelphia: Westminster, 1957.

Williams 1962
Williams, G. H. *The Radical Reformation,* Philadelphia: Westminster, 1962.

Wray 1954
Wray, F. J. "The Anabaptist Doctrine of the Restitution of the Church," *MQR* 28 (1954), 186-96.

Wray 1956
Wray, F. J. "The 'Vermanung' of 1542 and Rothmann's 'Bekenntnisse,'" *ARG* 47 (1956), 243-51.

WPM
The Writings of Pilgram Marpeck, transl. & ed. W. Klassen and W. Klaassen, Scottdale: Herald Press, 1978.

Yoder 1973
The Legacy of Michael Sattler, ed. J. H. Yoder, Scottdale: Herald Press, 1973.

Zeschwitz 1881
Zeschwitz, C. A. von. *Das mittelalterliche Drama vom Ende des römischen Kaisertums deutscher Nation, und von der Erscheinung des Antichrists,* Nach einer Tegernseer Handschrift des zwölften Jahrhunderts, nebst deutscher Übersetzung, Leipzig, 1881.

Ziegler 1969
Ziegler, D. J. ed. *Great Debates of the Reformation*, New York: Random House, 1969.

Scripture Index

Name and Subject Index